U0896079

《云南少数民族非纸质典籍聚珍·金石器物类》编委会名单

国家民文出版项目库项目

民族文字出版专项资金资助项目

云南少数民族非纸质典籍聚珍

云南省少数民族古籍整理出版规划办公室◎编

金石器物类

和六花◎主编

云南出版集团
云南人民出版社

图书在版编目（CIP）数据

云南少数民族非纸质典籍聚珍 . 金石器物类 / 云南省少数民族古籍整理出版规划办公室编 ; 和六花主编 . -- 昆明 : 云南人民出版社 , 2020.1
ISBN 978-7-222-16920-3

Ⅰ . ①云… Ⅱ . ①云… ②和… Ⅲ . ①少数民族—古籍—汇编—云南 Ⅳ . ① K280.74

中国版本图书馆 CIP 数据核字 (2018) 第 260395 号

出 品 人：李　维　赵石定
责任编辑：金学丽　雷敢星
封面设计：马　滨
责任校对：沈正德
民文校对：岩满叫（傣文）　王明富（壮文）　旦正太（藏文）
责任印制：代隆参

云南少数民族非纸质典籍聚珍 · 金石器物类
YUNNAN SHAOSHU MINZU FEIZHIZHI DIANJI JUZHEN · JINSHI QIWU LEI
云南省少数民族古籍整理出版规划办公室◎编
和六花◎主编

出版　云南出版集团　云南人民出版社
发行　云南人民出版社
社址　昆明市环城西路 609 号
邮编　650034
网址　www.ynpph.com.cn
E-mail　ynrms@sina.com
开本　889mm × 1194mm　1/16
印张　17.25
版次　2020 年 1 月第 1 版第 1 次印刷
印刷　重庆新金雅迪艺术印刷有限公司
书号　ISBN 978-7-222-16920-3
定价　560.00 元

云南人民出版社
微信公众号

如有图书质量及相关问题请与我社联系
审校部电话：0871-64164626　印制科电话：0871-64191534

概说

我国是一个统一的多民族国家。在漫长的历史发展进程中，各民族创造并积累了丰富多彩的历史文化，留下了浩如烟海的古籍。这些古籍资料，从不同的角度记录中华各民族的社会进程、历史走向和文化内涵，从不同侧面反映各民族祖先的智慧、文明成果和气质风貌，是中华文化的重要组成部分，是文化传承的独特载体，是中华民族多元一体格局的真实映射。少数民族古籍是其中不可或缺、独具特色的重要部分。云南素有“民族文化博物馆”之美誉，各民族先民创造了卷帙浩繁的书面文献和难以计数的口传文献。这些少数民族古籍涉及的语言文种多种多样，记录的内容博大精深，载体形态更是纷繁复杂，有记载历史时期官方盟誓、功绩、先贤德行、颁赏、封诰等的金石铭刻，有描绘先民生产生活景致和认知的岩画，有刻写了经书、经文和神灵造像的石刻，有绘制于麻布之上的各民族信仰的神灵造像，有用铁笔刻写在贝多罗树叶上的贝叶经，等等。这些便是本套丛书所要收集、采录的少数民族非纸质典籍。

一

中国少数民族古籍（以下简称少数民族古籍），是指中国55个少数民族在历史上用各自的语言文字形成的文献典籍、碑刻铭文和口头传承资料等。其内容涉及政治、哲学、历史、宗教、军事、文学、艺术、语言文字、地理、天文历算、经济、医学等领域。本套丛书收集、采录的少数民族古籍的时间范畴一般以1911年为下限，但由于各民族的历史特点和古籍存世情况差异，根据各民族古籍的实际情况，有的可以延伸到1949年。

少数民族古籍是中国传统文化的重要组成部分，是古籍学、文献学的重要研究对象。过去，传统研究未对此作出全面、系统的阐述，直到20世纪80年代，随着各级各类民族古籍工作部门的建立，民族古籍工作迎来了春天。1981年中共中央在《关于整理我国古籍的指示》中指出："整理古籍，把祖国宝贵的文化遗产继承下来，是一项十分重要的、关系到子孙后代的工作。"1984年，国务院在转发《国家民委关于抢救、整理少数民族古籍的请示》的通知中强调："少数民族古籍是祖国宝贵文化遗产的一部分，抢救、整理少数民族古籍，是一项十分重要的工作。"根据指示精神，从国家到地方都建立了相应的民族古籍工作部门，全面开展少数民族古籍的抢救保护、整理出版工作。我国少数民族古籍工作以"救书、救人、救学科"为己任，取得了丰硕的成果。然而，这项工作也面临着重重困难，走得异常艰难。随着社会日新月异的发展，少数民族古籍资源和古籍人才流失态势日趋严峻，少数民族古籍学科的发展又相对滞后，基础理论研究十分薄弱。诸如，中国各少数民族古籍种类众多、卷帙浩繁，对于少数民族古籍的分类至今仍无定论。对"民族古籍"的界定，是一个非常重要的问题，观点众说纷纭[①]。这里，我们无意对此做系统梳理，只为明确少数民族非纸质典籍收录的范围。

在少数民族古籍抢救保护、整理出版工作中，特别是1997年以来，围绕《中国少数民族古籍总目提要》开展的全国范围内的少数民族古籍整理工作中，我们习惯性地将民族古籍主要分为两大类：一是有文字类；二是无文字类。有文字类的民族古籍又包括三个子类：一是用各少数民族文字及少数民族古文字记载的历史文书和历史典籍；二是用汉文记载的有关少数民族内容的古代文献典籍；三是用少数民族文字和汉文记载的有关少数民族

① 李国文在《云南少数民族古籍文献调查与研究》（民族出版社2010年版）一书的前言中对学界关于"民族古籍"的理解和界定做了较为系统的回顾。近年，也有相关研究做了一些讨论，观点几乏善可陈。

内容的碑刻铭文。无文字的民族古籍主要是指各少数民族在历史上口头传承下来的具有历史和文化价值的各种资料[①]。在《中国少数民族古籍总目提要》实施过程中，鉴于少数民族古籍文献载体形式的不同，又将少数民族古籍细分为书籍类、铭刻类、文书类和讲唱类四类予以收录[②]。其中，书籍类全面收录少数民族在历史上形成的具有古典装帧形式的书册。铭刻类收录石碑、摩崖石刻、墓志、鼎彝、哀册、金属刻、竹木刻等碑刻铭文。文书类收录各类告示、契约、传单、函告、函件、账单、抄件、公约、规章、执照、档案、书信、柬帖等文献资料。讲唱类则收录少数民族口头传承的有关民族起源、民族迁徙、文明起源等具有历史文化价值的神话、传说、故事、歌谣等。依据少数民族古籍文献载体产生的四分类法，用于《中国少数民族古籍总目提要》各民族卷的编撰是符合客观实际且行之有效的。与此同时，因此项工作涉及面广、持续时间较长，这个分类法影响力较大。但是，依据古籍的载体形式对民族古籍加以分类，可否将“文书类”单独归为一类尚可斟酌。何谓“文献载体”？《辞海》中对于“载体”一词给出了五层解释，其中一个“指承载知识或信息的物质形体”。顾名思义，“文献载体”就是文献的物质载体，纸、绢帛、布匹、木头、树叶、兽骨、石头、金石器物、兽皮等等都可作为文献载体。“文书”一词起源甚早，早在汉晋时期的史籍中即已出现，是指以文字为主要方式记录信息的一种书面文书，按其性质可分为对公文书和对私文书，各类告示、契约、传单、函告、函件、账单、抄件、公约、规章、执照、档案、书信、柬帖等皆属文书。从这个层面来说，文书是依照文献内容界定的概念。在云南少数民族古籍中，同为文书，也有不同的物质载体形式，有书写在纸上的，有凿刻在砖石上的。

此外，乌谷先生《民族古籍》一书对民族古籍的概念及其分类颇具代表性，他认为：“民族古籍就是指曾经在中华人民共和国疆域范围内生活过的各少数民族或正在生活着的各少数民族在历史上遗留下来的一切用文字、具有某种文化含义的符号（文字的雏形）及口头语言记录下来的文化载体。这种文化载体可分为四大类型，即原生载体古籍、金石载体古籍、口碑载体古籍和书面载体古籍。”[③]按照乌谷先生的分类，各民族在历史上留传下来的以竹简、布帛、纸张为载体的各种历史文献，包括用各种民族文字书写出来的书籍、

---

① 国家民族事务委员会全国少数民族古籍整理研究室：《中国少数民族古籍总目提要·纳西族卷》“序言”，中国大百科全书出版社 2003 年版。

② 国家民族事务委员会全国少数民族古籍整理研究室：《中国少数民族古籍总目提要·哈尼族卷》“序言”，中国大百科全书出版社 2008 年版，第 10 页。

③ 乌谷：《民族古籍学》，云南民族出版社 1994 年版，第 6 页。

档案、文书、诏令、户籍、契约、谱牒、信札、告示、乡规民约等都归为书面载体古籍。而在众多的分类法中，铭刻类（或称金石载体古籍）、讲唱类（或称口碑古籍）按载体形式作为单独的一类没有太多的争议。但“铭刻类”和“金石载体古籍”因提法不同，内涵和外延产生了很大的差异，铭刻类涉及的物质载体更为宽泛、全面，不局限于金石器物，涵盖了石刻、竹木刻、骨刻、摩崖、器物等，铭刻类实质上已涵盖乌谷先生所界定的书面载体古籍和原生载体古籍的一部分，但“铭刻类”强调的是古籍的书写方式，而非载体形式。“金石载体古籍”这个类目的界定又略显狭隘，未将骨刻、竹木刻等载体形式囊括其中。乌谷先生虽另外界定了“原生载体”这个类目，“原生载体是指在一个民族的文字形成之初，用于记事表意被赋予某种特殊涵义的实物或符号。……我国各民族在自己的历史上都曾先后留下了大量有关刻木记事、结绳记事、实物记事等生动翔实的原生载体古籍。”[①]从这个概念来看，将骨刻、竹木刻归入原生载体古籍一类显然不合适。

综上所述，因中国各少数民族所处的环境不同、历史发展进程各异，少数民族古籍的载体形式多种多样，有的数量稀少却异常珍贵，有的历史上有过却早已佚失。用一种或者几种载体类别对琳琅纷呈的中国少数民族古籍作分类，难度巨大，难免挂一漏万，概括不够全面。我们选择以“非纸质”作为切入点，除了纸质载体以外的，具有有形实物载体的云南少数民族古籍都是我们收录的对象，意在将散布在各地图书馆、博物馆、档案馆等馆藏机构的以及散藏民间的，长期未公之于众的，又具有重要历史文化价值、文物价值和科学研究价值的云南各少数民族非纸质载体古籍汇编成册，公开出版发行。

二

云南是一个多民族聚居的省份，人口达5000人以上的世居少数民族有25个，除回族、水族、满族3个少数民族已通用汉语外，其余22个少数民族使用着26种语言（有的民族使用两种或两种以上语言），其中14个民族拥有23种文字或拼音方案（有的民族使用两种或两种以上文字），并留下了卷帙浩繁的民族古籍。据统计，云南散藏民间的藏文古籍、纳西东巴古籍、彝文古籍、壮文古籍、傈僳族音节文字古籍、白文古籍、普米族韩规古籍、傣文古籍、瑶文古籍等计有10万余册（卷）。其他如哈尼族、苗族、拉祜族、佤族、景颇族、布朗族、布依族、阿昌族、怒族、基诺族、德昂族、水族、独龙族等虽无本民族的古老文字，

① 乌谷：《民族古籍学》，云南民族出版社1994年版，第10页。

但他们靠口耳相传传承本民族历史文化，口传文献丰富多彩，创世史诗、迁徙史诗、叙事长诗、神话、传说、祭祀歌、劳动歌、生活习俗歌等数以万计。此外，有古老文字的民族中尚有大量口传文献流传。云南少数民族口传古籍达4万余种，内容涉及政治、哲学、法律、历史、宗教、军事、文学、艺术、语言、文字、地理、天文、历算、经济、医学等领域。

云南少数民族古籍储量巨大、历史悠久、载体多样，其中不乏非纸质典籍。依据现有资料来看，云南25个世居少数民族都或多或少拥有一些非纸质典籍。每一个民族都曾经历过或正在经历着无文字的历史阶段，为便于沟通交流、传辞达意，随之萌芽了一些可用于记事表意的"实物语言"或"符号语言"，如结绳记事、刻木记事、树叶信等原生文化载体。在特殊文化场阈中，这些原生文化载体被赋予不同的象征意义，随着人类社会的发展，特别是文字产生后，原生文化载体在群体中的实用价值逐渐被淡化，有的甚至消失在了历史长河中。但在无文字民族中，这些原生文化载体的实用价值已远超其文化和文物价值。原生文化载体是否能纳入民族古籍的范畴，至今仍众说纷纭。鉴于云南各少数民族留存至今的原生文化载体数量不多，且新近发现者居多，族属难辨、释读不易，本书未做收录。在目前所知的十余万册云南少数民族古籍中，基于各民族分布区自然环境各异，历史发展进程各有轨迹，传统文化各具特色，民族古籍的载体可谓琳琅满目，布匹、竹木、兽骨、兽皮、金石器物等都在不同的历史时期成为不同族群古籍的承载体。这里，我们大体介绍一下非纸质典籍数量较多、载体较具代表性的几个民族的古籍情况：

1. 纳西族典籍

目前已知国内外收藏的东巴古籍有1000余种（内容大体相同的算为一种）3万余册，俗称"东巴经"，多数为图画象形文字写本，部分为图画象形文和哥巴文掺杂写本，极少数为纯哥巴文写本。其以宗教典籍为主，亦包括用东巴文书写的文书、铭刻和纳西族口耳相传的口头文献，内容涵盖社会历史、语言文字、哲学宗教、风俗习惯、文学艺术、天文医学等多方面，被誉为"纳西族古代社会的百科全书"。按其内容可分为祈福延寿类的《远祖回归记》《献牲》《神鹏和署争斗的故事》等，禳鬼消灾类的《鲁般鲁饶》《董术战争》《创世纪》《白蝙蝠取经记》等，丧葬超度类的《杀猛鬼和恩鬼，高勒趣招父魂》《人类迁徙的来历》《马的来历》等，占卜类的《大地上卜卦之书》《用巴格图占卜》《占梦之书》等，涉及舞蹈、医药、民歌等的《东巴舞谱》《医药之书》《民歌范本》等，以及独具地域特色的丽江市宁蒗彝族自治县油米村的阮可东巴经。

纳西族非纸质典籍中，最具代表性、使用最广泛、储量较多的，有绘制于木头之上的木牌画和布匹之上的卷轴画。木牌画是一种历史悠久的原始绘画艺术，是东巴艺术在萌芽阶段的作品，大多应用于大型祭祀活动。木牌一般长约 60 厘米、宽约 10 厘米、厚约 1 厘米，内容依照东巴画谱所记载的为准，按祭祀功能可分为神牌、鬼牌、门牌、还债牌、诅咒牌等。图像造型奇特，形貌古朴，线条粗犷，笔法豪放，自然流畅，具有先民原始艺术的特点。卷轴画，纳西语叫“普劳幛”，是东巴用矿物质颜料绘制于土布上的神像画，是东巴绘画艺术跨入发达阶段而趋于精熟的作品，有长卷、多幅和独幅等多种。每幅卷轴画主要画一尊大神或护法神，表现某个神祇及其所居的神界，用于东巴教仪式中，悬挂于神坛正上方，不同仪式所挂的神像不尽相同。具有代表性的卷轴画有东巴教教主东巴什罗像、东巴教大神依古窝格、战神优麻、阳神董神、阴神术神、萨依威德、神路图等。其中，神路图是东巴卷轴画中最原始、最有代表性的巨作，一般宽 16~30 厘米、长约 15 米。画卷分段连续描绘地狱、人间、天堂三个部分，绘有 360 多个人、神、鬼及 70 多种奇禽怪兽，被称为我国美术史上最长的直幅长卷，享有“古代宗教绘画第一长卷”之誉，具有较高的文化和艺术研究价值。神路图的内容、性质、用途大体一致，但因载体材质、颜料、绘画技法等不同，每一幅神路图都有独特的艺术风格。

2. 壮族古籍

壮族有自己的语言文字，壮语属汉藏语系壮侗语族壮傣语支，分南北两大方言。壮族文字在先秦时期即已萌芽，隋唐时期，壮族先民即用汉字记壮语，效仿汉字六书的构字方法创制了方块壮字，称“土字”或“土俗字”，并用古壮字来记录民间故事，书写经文、家谱、碑文、账务等，一批方块壮字古籍流传至今。古壮文古籍，壮语称“师摩”“师多在”“师雅”等，“师”壮语意为“书籍”，多抄写在用纱皮树树皮制成的纱纸上，或是用嫩竹、构树皮制成的者卡土纸上。壮族古籍种类广、数量多，有记录摩教仪式、经文、教义的《摩经布洛陀》《摩荷泰》《麻仙》《德傣掸登俄》等，有反映朴素世界观和价值观的叙事长诗、古歌，如《盘古歌》《卜伯》《摩则杜》等，有民间七言叙事诗《毛洪》《董永》《舜儿》等，亦不乏展现绘画艺术的《鸡卜经》及宗教绘画“莱摩”，内容涉及历史、语言、文学、艺术、哲学、宗教、天文、历算等众多方面，可谓博大精深、绮丽多姿。

壮族的非纸质典籍以岩画、骨刻书和绘画典籍较具代表性。一是岩画。今壮族分布区尚存数百处摩崖石刻。据现有考古资料，今壮族分布区有众多的原始刻绘艺术遗存，虽难于明确界定这些考古遗存的族属，但壮族先民是这些绘画遗存的创作者、拥有者之一是确信无疑的。分布在文山壮族苗族自治州境内最具代表性的岩画，有麻栗坡大王岩岩画、丘北黑箐龙岩画、砚山卡子岩画、广南弄卡岩画、西畴蚌谷狮子山岩画等10余处，占地约5430平方米，有170幅400多个图案。二是骨刻书。云南壮族先民在器物、兽骨甚至身体上刻绘图案的历史由来已久，至今仍在部分地区传承使用，其中以壮族的骨刻历算器最为著名，文山壮族苗族自治州民族宗教事务委员会即在境内发现58块骨刻。骨刻，壮语称“甲巴克”“瓦甲巴”，意为刻在骨片上的图纹符号、书籍，是原始先民推算日历、占卜的器具。兽骨上一般刻有人物、桌子、棺材、植物、弓箭、动物、干栏、太阳纹等图像，是一种兼具审美和记事功能的图像文字。三是神像画。壮族神像画众多，类型多样、作品丰富，隐含借“神”避邪的世俗观念，审美态度与情感交织。依据其内容、形制、用途，大体分为摩教神图长卷、宗教挂图和占卜绘画三类。其中，摩教神图长卷是摩教特有的宗教神图之一，由摩教祭司传承使用；绘于壮族自制土麻布上，形制为长卷竖幅，分栏作画，多用于丧葬仪式、祭扫仪式等。

3. 傣族古籍

傣族有本民族文字。傣文古籍多为刻本、写本、稿本和抄本，有贝叶古籍和纸质（绵纸、构皮纸）古籍两种，形制一般为梵夹装、经折装、线装，主要流传于西双版纳、德宏、保山、普洱、临沧、红河等州市的傣族地区。按内容大致有宗教类的《朗丝奢不仙宰》《杀鸡祭水神祷辞》《祭谷魂词》《招魂词》等，政治历史类的《泐史》《孟连宣抚史》等，文学艺术类的《巴塔麻嘎捧尚罗》《兰嘎西贺》《厘俸》，以及天文历法类、农田水利类、医药类、理论专著类、军事武术类、语言文字类、译著类等。

傣族的非纸质典籍载体多样、数量众多，最具代表性的便是傣族的银器、贝叶经书和绘画典籍。其中，贝叶经是最具代表性的非纸质典籍。贝叶经，傣语称作“坦兰”，是用民间制作的铁笔刻写在经过特制的贝多罗树叶上而成的。此外，傣族的壁画、布画等非纸质绘画典籍也较有特色。

4. 彝族古籍

彝族有自己的语言和文字。语言属汉藏语系藏缅语族彝语支，可分为东部、西部、南部、北部、中部、东南部六大方言区。彝族有自己古老的文字，汉文古籍称其为“夷经”“爨文”“罗罗文”等，现统称老彝文，每一个字形代表一个字义，并有不同写法。现存的老彝文有1万多字形，常用的有1000多字。历史上，彝族先民用老彝文撰写了卷帙浩繁的文献典籍和数量众多的金石铭刻，内容涉及政治、军事、哲学、宗教、历史、地理、语言、文字、文学、艺术、天文、历算、医药、卫生等方面。近现代流行于彝族地区的彝文古籍主要有纸书、皮书、布书、骨书、岩书、瓦书、木牍、木刻、金石铭刻、印玺等载体形制，其中纸书占绝对比例，包括抄本与木刻印刷本两种。现存彝文古籍达2万余册（件），手抄本较多，少数为木刻印刷本。云南彝文古籍可分为滇南彝文古籍、武定禄劝彝文古籍、撒尼彝文古籍、阿哲彝文古籍、宣威彝文古籍、罗平彝文古籍、北部彝文古籍七类。较具代表性的有传统宗教礼仪典籍《吾查》《们查》《指路经》《祭龙经》《祈雨经》《鲁资楠道》《脑斯古》《招魂经》《尼布木司》等，著名文学作品有《阿诗玛》《尼迷诗》等，创世史诗有《查姆》《阿细的先基》《梅葛》《阿黑西尼摩》《尼苏夺节》等，译文文献长诗有《董永与七仙女》《凤凰记》《木荷与薇叶》《唐王游地府》《唐僧取经记》等。

云南彝族非纸质典籍最具代表性的是彝文摩崖。如昆明市禄劝彝族苗族自治县境内便有一通我国西南彝族地区历史较永久、留存较完整的长篇彝文金石铭刻——罗婺盛世史摩崖，刻面高206厘米 ×80厘米，镌刻于明嘉靖十年（1531年），迄今已有480多年，记述了武定凤氏土司14代350多年间的兴盛史。

云南每一个少数民族都拥有或者曾经拥有过或多或少的非纸质典籍。新中国成立以后特别是20世纪80年代后，很多的非纸质典籍得到了抢救保护，有的收藏于各级各类收藏机构，有的陈列于各类博物馆，有的已有了相关的整理研究成果。但更多的非纸质典籍，如深藏山野的摩崖石刻正经历着风吹日晒、沧海桑田，有的还曾经历过灭顶之灾；如壮族骨刻散布民间、无人释读，研究者有意寻访亦难见其真颜；又如纳西族木牌因仪式物品使用禁忌、用完即毁，难寻旧物……如此种种不止是云南少数民族非纸质典籍面临的生境，也是少数民族古籍所面临的困境。

三

文化是民族的根脉，是人类的精神家园，是一个民族凝聚力、生命力、创造力的源泉，是国家强盛的重要支撑。少数民族古籍真实而生动地记录了少数民族的历史发展进程，蕴含着少数民族特有的精神价值、思维方式和非凡的想象力、创造力，是人类文明的瑰宝，是中国珍贵的文化遗产。在长期的传播交流过程中，少数民族古籍发挥着积极进取的价值取向和经世致用的社会功能。一部优秀的民族古籍作品，其在民族社会中的价值远远超出了一个学科的专业范畴，代表了一个民族在某个专业领域的认知、反映了一个民族的某个历史发展阶段，甚或承载、再现了一个民族的社会事实和历史走向。加强少数民族古籍抢救和保护，对于丰富中华文化宝库，全面了解中华民族的发展历程，构建平等团结互助和谐的社会主义新型民族关系，推动民族团结进步事业，具有重要的历史意义和现实意义。

中华人民共和国成立后，在各级党委、政府的领导下，经过几代古籍工作者筚路蓝缕的努力，云南省少数民族古籍抢救保护和翻译整理出版工作取得了显著成绩。本着“抢救为主，保护第一”的原则，抢救了少数民族文字文献古籍3万余册（卷），口传古籍1万余种，以《纳西东巴古籍译注全集》《中国贝叶经全集》《彝族毕摩经典译注全集》《云南少数民族古籍珍本集成》《红河彝族文化遗产古籍典藏》《云南少数民族古典史诗全集》《云南少数民族叙事长诗全集》等为代表的民族古籍抢救保护成果引起国内外的广泛关注。但是，于卷帙浩繁的少数民族古籍而言，目前的抢救保护、翻译整理成果不过是沧海一粟。初略估算，除已征集保管的少数民族古籍以外，云南仍有7万余册（卷）的少数民族文字文献古籍散存民间。由于保管不善或无人传承等诸多原因，许多散存民间的古籍难于做到活态传承，佚失、损毁现象严重，抢救保护迫在眉睫。就云南少数民族非纸质典籍而言，其生境尤令人担忧。部分可移动的、具有文物价值的非纸质古籍，多数已被各级各类机构、企业、私人征集收藏，这样的抢救保护最大化地彰显了此类古籍的文物价值，但这些民族古籍收而藏之后，原本在民间尚能活态传承的民族智慧结晶极易成为待在深闺无人识的宝贝；少量仍存于民间的，亦不乏寻访之人，各色寻访者在山乡村寨走访寻宝，有的甚至被倒卖流到境外。而诸多不可以移动的非纸质古籍的生境更是让人心生惋惜，这些承载着民族文化的石刻、摩崖多隐匿深山，常年经受着日晒雨淋以致文字符号或字迹模糊、难于辨识，或直接被人为损毁。石刻、摩崖受自然侵蚀逐渐消失，这是事物发展的自然规律，但对于民族文化而言是一个让人痛心的巨大损失。

我们在做这套丛书的过程中，也亲历和见证了数次痛心的时刻。2011年起，在云南省财政厅、云南省民族宗教事务委员会的支持下，我们一直在持续开展“云南省百项少数民族文化精品工程”项目《云南少数民族古籍珍本集成》。同时，按照《国家民委关于印发全国少数民族古籍保护工作“十三五”规划通知》的要求，“基本完成全国少数民族古籍普查工作。会同相关部门全力推进普查工作，摸清各地少数民族古籍资源。建立健全普查登记管理制度，构建普查登记平台，对各地少数民族古籍普查情况进行录入、统计、汇总，形成全国少数民族古籍普查登记目录档案”。本着“摸家底、建平台”的目的，我们在云南全省范围内开展了少数民族古籍普查、采录工作。为此，我们访遍云南各州市的少数民族古籍收藏机构，走访古籍传承人、收藏爱好者，足迹几遍及云南全省。2016年，我们在迪庆藏族自治州调研时，迪庆藏族自治州藏学研究院的同志为我们介绍了州内非纸质典籍的留存分布情况，提到在维西傈僳族自治县塔城镇附近一个山坡上有很多藏文石刻。我们在电脑里看到了该院数年前实地调研时拍摄的照片，从中可以看到半面山坡都是石刻，都是一些有些年代的文化遗存。我们异常兴奋，因为这个石刻分布地和发现唐代藏文碑刻《格子碑》的格子村相距仅数里，又隐匿深山，难保不是一些有价值的非纸质典籍。遗憾的是，因此行我们未携带拍摄设备，心想留待日后再专程前来调研。未想此次擦肩而过，却错失了一睹其风采的机会。2018 年 5 月，我们组织了专业的拍摄、传拓人员前往迪庆州，一行人在迪庆州藏学院相关同志的带领下，经历修路堵车、徒步山林，风尘仆仆地来到那片山坡。可眼前的景象却让我们傻眼了，哪里还见得到石刻，只见坡头有一道高五六米的混着石头的土堆，下方红土里稀稀拉拉种了一些重楼。几经周折联系上村委会的同志，方得知该村为发展农业经济，特地请了推土机来平整了土地，这些石刻已经被埋到了土堆下。这只是我们在开展云南少数民族古籍抢救保护工作中经历的几乎不值一提的一件小事，这样的事情不止在迪庆，在全省各地都在发生着；不止石刻、摩崖，纸质文献、丝帛素书、竹木简牍无不面临着这样的生存困境。倾心于民族文化抢救保护的人们深感痛心疾首，却也深深地感受到，仅凭一个部门、一些群体去抢救保护，确实是势单力薄。基于这样的现状，抢救保护非纸质典籍确实是迫在眉睫。基于经费、人员、技术等各方面的制约，哪怕是采用最简单、最传统的办法，先把这些文化遗存的影像留下来，供社会科学研究使用，同时呼吁全社会共同关注民族古籍的抢救保护，这是一件意义深远的事情，也是本丛书策划之初最真实的出发点。

长期以来，云南人民出版社对云南少数民族古籍的抢救保护、整理出版工作给予了极大的支持。2016 年，将云南少数民族非纸质典籍抢救保护项目申报国家民族文字图书出版资金资助。云南省少数民族古籍整理出版规划办公室于数年前就多次到民族地区征集典籍，了解线索，拍摄图片。经过数年的努力，由丽江市博物院、丽江东巴文化研究院、丽江市玉龙纳西族自治县图书馆等单位和一些民间收藏爱好者收藏的云南非纸质典籍最终得以在此书中整合出版。为收集这些非纸质典籍，相关人员付出了辛勤劳动，足迹几遍及云南全省。大量的原数据采集回来后，我们在典籍的分类整合上却遇到了前所未有的困难。云南各少数民族的非纸质典籍载体可谓琳琅满目，每种载体类型古籍的数量和质量参差不齐，作为丛书汇总出版既要全面涵盖具有代表性的非纸质典籍的载体类型，又要兼顾覆盖各民族的非纸质典籍；既要鉴别甄选各民族非纸质典籍的珍品、精品，又要尽可能地考虑民族古籍在民族社会中的情感价值；既要客观地收录古籍珍品，又要考虑每卷图书的体量和规模。几经求证，严格按照民族古籍学的学科分类对云南的非纸质典籍进行归类，几乎是不可能的。我们只能对倾尽全力收集到的非纸质典籍做个大概的分类，各卷再细分类目。少数民族古籍的抢救保护是一项长期的工作，不是朝夕之功。我们想全面呈现云南非纸质典籍的精品、珍品，在实际工作中会不断发现新典籍、扩充新的类目，所以丛书难免有不当之处，唯有祈求方家海涵、指正。

总的说来，本丛书是云南少数民族非纸质典籍的第一次集成和汇总。它将以往秘不外传的众多少数民族古籍珍品第一次集中展示于世人面前，不论学术价值、史料价值，还是传世、鉴赏、收藏价值等都具有诸多独特性，在保护各民族文化遗产、弘扬各民族优秀文化、增进民族团结、促进中华民族共有精神家园建设等方面具有重要意义。

General Introduction

China is a unified multi-ethnic country. Various ethnic minorities have created and accumulated rich and colorful historic culture, while leaving a vast number of ancient books and records in the process of long-term historical development. Recording social process, historical trends and cultural connotations from different perspectives and reflecting wisdom, civilization achievements and the essence style from various sides, these ancient books and records are an important part of Chinese culture, a unique carrier for cultural inheritance, and a real reflection of the diversified but integrated historical pattern in China. Ancient books and records of ethnic minorities are an indispensable and unique part. Yunnan has long been enjoying the good reputation as "Museum of Ethnic Culture". Ancestors of ethnic minorities have created voluminous written documents and countless oral literature. A great diversity of language record types are involved in the ancient books of ethnic minorities. The contents of the records are extensive and profound, and the carrier forms are more complicated. Besides, there are inscriptions recording the historical events such as the official vows, merits and achievements, virtues of ancient wise men, awarding and imperial mandate appointments. Moreover, there are cliff engravings carved on the cliffs to depict the production and living situations as well as the cognitions of the ancestors. There are also sutras and scriptures carved in stone, stone-carved statues of gods, and Pattra-leaf Scriptures carved on pattra leaves with the stencil pen (a cutting tool used in carving seals, etc.). These are the non-paper ancient books and records of ethnic minorities to be collected and recorded in this series of book.

I

Ancient books and records of ethnic minorities in China (hereinafter referred to as ancient books and records of ethnic minorities) refer to ancient books and records, inscriptions, oral inheritance materials and other documents of 55 ethnic minorities in their respective languages in history, contents of which cover politics, philosophy, history, religion, military affairs, literature, art, languages, geography, the celestial almanac, economy, medicine and other fields. 1911 is generally taken as the lower limit for the time category of ancient books and records of ethnic minorities. However, due to historical characteristics of various ethnic minorities and differences in the existence of the ancient books and records, some of them may be extended to 1949 in accordance with the actual situation of ancient books of various ethnic minorities.

Ancient books and records of ethnic minorities are an important part of Chinese traditional culture as well as an important study subject of ancient books, records and literature. In the past, there were no comprehensive or systematic explanations on such subject in the traditional research. Nevertheless, with the establishment of various levels and kinds of departments on ancient books of ethnic minorities in the 1980s, work of ancient books and records of ethnic minorities ushered in the spring. In 1981, the Central Committee of the Communist Party of China pointed out in *The Instructions on Sorting-out of Ancient Chinese Books* that "it is a fundamental task that affects later generations to sort out ancient books and records and inherit the precious cultural heritage of the nation." The State Council, in forwarding the notification of *The Request from the State Civil Affairs Commission on the Rescue and Sorting-out of Ancient Books and Records of Ethnic Minorities,* stressed that "ancient books and records of ethnic minorities are part of the precious cultural heritage of the nation, and it is a fundamental task to rescue and to sort-out them" in 1984. In accordance with the instructions, corresponding departments responsible for the work of ancient books and records of ethnic minorities were set up at the national and local levels to carry out the rescue, protection, sorting-out and publication of ancient books of ethnic minorities. Over the three decades past, relevant personnel responsible for ancient books and records of ethnic minorities have been taking the mission of "rescuing books, people and disciplines" as their mission, and achieved fruitful goals. However, this task is also faced with numerous difficulties, and it is extremely difficult to push it forward. With the rapid development of society, depletion of ancient book and record resources and the outflow of talents for ancient books and records of ethnic minorities become increasingly severe. Besides, the development of the discipline on ancient books and records of ethnic minorities is relatively backward, and the basic theoretical research is very weak. For instance, there are so many voluminous ancient books and records of ethnic minorities in China that the classification of such books is still inconclusive. Moreover, the definition of "ethnic ancient books and records" is a very important issue, but relevant opinions are divergent. [1] Here, we have no intention to make systematical sorting, but just to clarify the inclusion scope of non-paper ancient books and records of ethnic minorities.

During the rescue, protection, sorting-out and publication of ancient books and records of ethnic minorities, especially since 1997, when sorting out ancient books and records of ethnic minorities conducted throughout the country on *Summary of the Catalog of Ancient Books and Records of Chinese Ethnic Minorities*, we habitually divide ethnic ancient books and records into two categories: literal and non-literal categories. Ethnic ancient books and records of literal category can be divided into the following three subcategories: first, historical documents, books and records recorded in the current and ancient languages of ethnic minorities. Secondly, ancient literature, books and records relevant to the ethnic minorities recorded in Chinese. Thirdly, inscriptions related to the ethnic minorities recorded in the Chinese and minority languages. Ethnic ancient books and records of non-literal category mainly refer to various kinds of historical and cultural documents handed down orally by the ethnic minorities in history. [2] In view of the different carrier forms, ancient books and records of ethnic minorities were further divided into four categories of books, inscriptions, documents as well as lectures and songs in the implementation of *Summary of the Catalog of Ancient Books and Records of Ethnic Minorities in China*. [3] Among them, the classical binding forms of books and records of ethnic minorities in history are comprehensively included in the category of books; stone-tablet and cliff carvings, epigraphs, inscriptions carved on the sacrificial utensil, the elegy volume, and bamboo and wooden engravings are included in the category of inscriptions. Various kinds of notices, contracts, leaflets, letters of notifications, correspondence, bills, duplicates,

---

① In the preface of *Investigation and Research on Ancient Books and Records of Ethnic Minorities in Yunnan* (The Ethnic Publishing House, Edition 2010), Li Guowen made a systematic review of the understanding and definition of "ancient books and records of ethnic minorities" in the academic circle. In recent years, there have been some discussions on the relevant research, but the views have nothing to brag about.

② The Research Office of Ancient Books and Records of Ethnic Minorities for National Ethnic Affairs Commission: "Preface" of *Volume of the Naxi Ethnic Group for Summary of Catalogue of Ancient Books and Records of Ethnic Minorities in China*, Edition 2003 by Encyclopedia of China Publishing House.

③ The Research Office of Ancient Books and Records of Ethnic Minorities for National Ethnic Affairs Commission: "Preface" of *Volume of the Hani Ethnic Group for Summary of Catalogue of Ancient Books and Records of Ethnic Minorities in China*, Page 10 of Edition 2008 by Encyclopedia of China Publishing House.

conventions, regulations, licenses, archives, letters, notes and other documents are included in the documentary category of ethnic ancient books and records. The myths, legends, stories and ballads with historical and cultural value related to ethnic origin, migration of ethnic minorities and the origin of civilization and other oral inheritance of ethnic minorities are included in the category of lectures and songs. According to the four-classification method of the literature carriers of ancient books and records of ethnic minorities, the compilation of various ethnic volumes in *Summary of the Catalog of Ancient Books and Records of Ethnic Minorities in China* is in line with the objective reality and effective. Meanwhile, the classification method has great influence because of the wide scope and long duration of the task. Nevertheless, since ethnic ancient books and records are classified according to the carrier forms, whether books and records of "documentary category" can be taken as an individual category is still to be considered. What is the "literature carrier"? Explanations in five aspects have been provided for the word "carrier", one of which refers to "the material form carrying knowledge or information". As the name suggests, "literature carrier" is the material carrier of literature. Materials such as paper, silk, cloth, wood, leaves, animal bones, stones, stone implements, and animal skins can be used as literature carriers. The word "document" can be dated far back in time, which could be seen in the historical records as early as in the Han and Jin Dynasties. Besides, it referred to a type of written documents taking the written language as the main method to record information, which could be divided into official and private documents, various kinds of notifications, contracts, leaflets, letter of notification, correspondence, bills, duplicates, conventions, regulations, licenses, archives, letters, notes and other documents by nature. Seen from this aspect, a document is a concept defined by the content of literature. In the ancient books and records of ethnic minorities in Yunnan, there are different forms of material carriers, such as documents written on paper or carved or chiseled on bricks and stones.

Furthermore, the concept and classification of ethnic ancient books and records mentioned in *Ethnic Ancient Books and Records* by Mr. Wu Gu were quite representative. He believed that "ethnic ancient books and records refer to all the cultural carriers of ethnic minorities who once lived or are living within the territory of the People's Republic of China, which are recorded in words, symbols with certain cultural meanings (prototypes of written language), and in oral languages carried over in history. This kind of cultural carriers can be divided into four major categories, i.e., ancient books and records of original, inscriptions, oral inheritance materials and written carriers." [1] According to the classification by Mr. Wu Gu, various kinds of historical documents passed on by the ethnic minorities in history with bamboo slips, cloth and paper as the carriers, including books, archives, documents, imperial edicts, household registrations, contracts, ultimatums, letters, notifications, township rules and folk contracts written in various ethnic languages, are classified as ancient books and records with written carriers. In the numerous classification methods, the category of inscriptions (or known as ancient books and records with ancient bronzes and stone tablet carriers) and the category of lectures and songs (or called as oral inheritance materials ancient books and records) can be regarded as separate categories according to the carrier form without many controversies. However, due to different names, the connotations and extensions of "inscriptions and ancient books and records with ancient bronze and stone tablet carriers" vary significantly. Inscriptions cover a broader and more comprehensive range of material carriers and are not restricted to stone implements, including stone, bamboo, wooden and bone carvings and cliff engravings, implements and other materials. In essence, the category of inscriptions covers part of the original carriers of ancient books and records as defined by Mr. Wu Gu. However, "inscriptions" emphasizes the writing modes of ancient books rather than the carrier forms. The category of "ancient books and records with carriers of ancient bronzes and stone tablets" is narrowly defined, which does not include such carrier forms as bone and bamboo carvings. Although Mr. Wu Gu further defined the category of "original carrier", "it referred to material objects or symbols provided with a certain special meaning and used to record events or express meanings at the beginning of formation of the written language of an ethnic minority... Each ethnic minority has left over a large number of vivid and detailed original ancient books and records relevant to record keeping of events through wooden carving, knot tying and record keeping with material objects." [2] Seen from this concept, it is obviously improper to classify bone, bamboo and wooden carvings into the ancient books and records with original carriers.

In conclusion, due to the different environments and historical development process of ethnic minorities in China, the carrier forms of ancient books and records of ethnic minorities are diverse. Some are rare but extremely precious, while some have disappeared in history. It is extremely difficult to classify the numerous ancient books and records of ethnic minorities in China with one or several carrier forms. Besides, it is hard to make comprehensive

① Wu Gu: *Studies on Ethnic Ancient Books and Records*, Edition 1994 by Yunnan Ethnic Publishing House, P6 .

② Wu Gu: *Studies on Ethnic Ancient Books and Records*, Edition 1994 by Yunnan Ethnic Publishing House , P10 .

generalizations. We choose the "non-paper" carrier forms as the point of penetration. In addition to paper carriers, ancient books and records with tangible physical carriers of ethnic minorities in Yunnan are all the objects to be included by us, for the purpose of compiling and publishing the ancient books with non-paper carriers of various ethnic minorities in Yunnan, which are scattered in libraries, museums, archive centers and other collection institutions in various regions, as well as the scattered folk collections, which have not been made public for a long time and have significant historical and cultural value, as well as value of cultural relics and scientific research.

II

Yunnan is a province where multiple ethnic minorities live in compact communities. 25 ethnic minorities with a population of more than 5,000 people have been living there for generations. Chinese is generally used in the three ethnic minorities (the Hui Ethnic minority, the Shui Ethnic minority and Manchu). However, the other 22 ethnic minorities use 26 languages (some ethnic minorities even use two or more languages). Among them, 14 ethnic minorities have 23 kinds of writing or spelling systems, and some of them use two or more written languages. Moreover, they have left over voluminous ethnic ancient books and records. According to the statistics, there are more than 100,000 books (volumes) of ancient books and records scattered in Yunnan, including those in Tibetan, Naxi Dongba, Yi, Zhuang characters, Lisu and Bai characters, Hangui characters in the Pumi Ethnic Minority, and Dai and Yao characters. As for other ethnic minorities such as the Hani, the Miao, he Lahu, the Wa, the Jingpo, the Bulang, the Buyi, the Achang, the Nu, the Jinuo, the De'ang, the Shui and the Dulong Ethnic Minorities, although they don't have their own ancient languages, they pass on their historic culture orally, with rich and colorful oral documents. Moreover, there are tens of thousands of creation epics, migration epics, narrative poems, myths, legends, sacrifice songs, labor songs, living custom songs, etc. Furthermore, there are still a large number of oral literatures passed down among the ethnic minorities with ancient languages. There are over 40,000 kinds of oral ancient records passed on in the ethnic minorities Yunnan, covering politics, philosophy, law, history, religion, military affairs, literature, art, language, writing, geography, astronomy, calendar, economy, medicine and other fields.

The ancient books and records of ethnic minorities in Yunnan have been provided with the characteristics of huge reserves, long history and various carriers, among which there are lots of non-paper ancient books and records. All the ethnic minorities once experienced or are experiencing a period of history without written languages. In order to facilitate communication and convey meanings, some "material languages" or "symbol languages" that can be used to record events and convey meanings were created, for instance, the original cultural carriers such as record-keeping through knots tying, wood carving and with leaf letters. Under the special cultural circumstances, these original cultural carriers were provided with different symbolic meanings. With the development of human society, especially after the creation of the written languages, the practical value of the original cultural carriers in the groups is gradually diluted, and some even disappeared in history. However, the practical value of these original cultural carriers has far exceeded their cultural and historical-relic value. Whether the original cultural carriers can be included into the category of ethnic ancient books and records is still controversial. In view of the fact that the number of original cultural carriers retained in various ethnic minorities in Yunnan is limited, the majority of the carriers were discovered recently, and that it is difficult to distinguish their ethnic minority classification and make interpretations, they are not included in this book. Based on the different natural environment in the distribution areas of various ethnic minorities, the distinctive historical development process, and the unique traditional culture, it can be said that there are a wide variety of the carriers for the over 100,000 discovered ancient books and records of ethnic minorities in Yunnan. Cloths, bamboos, animal bones and skins, ancient bronzes and stone tablet implements and other materials have become the carriers of ancient books and records of various ethnic minorities in different historical periods. Here, we generally introduce the ancient books and records of several ethnic minorities with a large number of non-paper ancient books and records as well as the representative carriers.

1. Ancient Books and Records of the Naxi Ethnic Minority

Currently, there are more than 1,000 kinds (over 30,000 volumes) of Dongba ancient books and records collected at home and abroad (books of roughly the same contents are taken as one kind), commonly known as "Dongba Scriptures". Besides, most are pictorial hieroglyphic-writing transcripts; some are mixed with pictorial pictographs and Geba scripts; a very few are pure Geba scripts. There are mainly ancient religious books and records, and documents and inscriptions in Dongba characters, and oral documents passed down from mouth to mouth by the Naxi Ethnic Minority are also included. Contents of the Dongba ancient books and records cover social history, language, philosophy, religion, customs, literature and art, astronomy, medicine and other fields, which can be regarded as "the encyclopedia of the ancient Naxi Ethnic

Minority". According to the contents, the ancient books and records can be divided into the category of praying for prolonged life including *The Return of Remote Ancestors, Animal Sacrifice, Battle between the Great Roc and the Shu Synopsis*, the category of ghosts and disaster elimination such as *Luban Lurao, The War between the "Dong" and "Su"Tribes, The Creation, White Bat's Collection of Scriptures*, the category of the release of the souls from suffering in the funerals such as *Killing the Devil Ghost and Helpful Ghost, Gao Lequ Recall of Father's Soul, The Origin of Human Migration*, and *The Origin of Horses*, the category of divination such as *The Book of the Divination of the Earth, Divination with Hatem Bagato*, and *The Skills of Divination by Interpreting Dreams*, and the category concerning dance, medicine and folk songs such as *Dongba Dance Notation, The Book of Medicine*, and *the Model of Folk Songs*, as well as the Ruanke Dongba Scripture with unique regional features at Youmi Village in Ninglang County of Lijiang City.

Among the Naxi non-paper ancient books and records, the most representative, the most widely used and the most abundant ones are the wooden-plaque paintings on wooden plaques and the scroll paintings on cloth. As a kind of primitive painting art with a long history, the wooden-plaque paintings is a work of Dongba art in its infancy stage, which is mostly used in large-scale sacrificial activities. Generally, the wooden plaques are approximately 60 cm in length, 10 cm in width and 1 cm in thickness, and the contents are in accordance with the records of Dongba picture copybooks. According to the sacrificial functions, they can be divided into god and ghost plaques, door plates, debt-collecting, cursing and other plaques. The picture is peculiar in shape, simple in appearance, straightforward in line, and bold, natural and fluent in brushwork, which is provided with the primitive art characteristics of the ancestors. Scroll paintings, known as "Pulaozhang" in Naxi Language, are statues of gods painted on homespun cloth by Dongba people with mineral pigments, and are all works tending to be sophisticated when the Dongba paintings have entered a developed stage, including multiple types such as long scrolls, multiple and single pieces. A great god or guardian god is mainly depicted in each scroll painting representing a certain god and the divine circle where it lived. The painting is used in Dongba religious rituals and directly hung above the altar. Different statues of gods are hung in different ceremonies. Representative scroll paintings include statues of Dingbasheluo (founder of the Dongba Religion), Yiguwoge (great god of the Dongba Religion), Youma (god of wars), God Dong (god of Yang), God Shu (god of Yin), Sayiweide and Road Maps of Gods. Among them, the painting of the road to heaven are the most original and representative masterpiece in Dongba scroll paintings, with a width of 16~30 cm and a length of approximately 15 meters. Three parts of the hell,the world of mortals and the heaven are successively depicted on the scroll paintings, with more than 360 individuals, gods, ghosts and over 70 kinds of odd birds and monsters. It is known as the longest straight scroll in the history of the Chinese art, and enjoys the reputation of "the first long scroll of the ancient religious painting", which is provided with high cultural and artistic research value. The contents, nature and use of road maps of gods are basically consistent. However, due to different carrier materials, pigments and painting techniques, each the painting of the road to heaven has its unique artistic style.

2. Ancient Books and Records of the Zhuang Ethnic Minority

The Zhuang Ethnic Minority has its own language and characters, and Zhuang Language is a category of the Zhuang-Dai language branch of the Zhuang-Dong Group of Sino-Tibetan Languages, divided into two big dialects of the north and south. Zhuang Language was already in the embryonic stage in the Pre-Qin Period. In the Sui and Tang Dynasties, ancestors of the Zhuang Ethnic Minority recorded Zhuang Language with Chinese characters, and invented the square Zhuang characters, called as "Tuzi"or "Tusuzi". Besides, they used ancient Zhuang characters to record folk stories, and record scriptures, genealogy, inscriptions, accounting, etc. Besides, a batch of ancient books in square Zhuang characters has been handed down. Ancient Zhuang books and records are known as "Shimo", "Shiduozai", "Shiya", etc. in Zhuang Language. "Shi" in Zhuang Language refers to "books", which are mainly transcribed on the gauze paper made of barks of the Shapi trees, written on the Zheka paper made from fresh bamboos or tapa. The ancient books of the Zhuang Ethnic Minority are in a wide variety and a large number, including books recording the rites, scriptures and doctrines of the Mo Religion such as *Buluotuo Lection, Mohetai, Maxian*, and *De Dai Shan Deng E*, narrative poems and ancient songs reflecting simplicity world view and values such as *Pangu Song, Bubo*, and *Mozedu*, folk seven-character narrative poems such as *Maohong, Dongyong* and *Shun'er*. Moreover, there are also quite a few *Jibu Scriptures* representing art of painting as well as the religious painting "Laimo", contents of which cover history, language, literature, art, philosophy, religion, astronomy, calendar and many other fields and can be said to be extensive and profound and gorgeous.

The non-paper ancient books and records of the Zhuang Ethnic Minority are represented by cliff engravings, bone carvings and drawing books and records. The first category is cliff engravings. There are hundreds of cliff engravings in the current distribution area of the Zhuang Ethnic Minority. According to the existing archaeological data, there are many original carved and painted art relics in the distribution area of today's Zhuang Ethnic Minority. Although it is difficult to clearly define the ethnic group of these archaeological relics, it is certain that the ancestors of the Zhuang Ethnic Minority are the creators and owners of these paintings. The most representative cliff engravings are distributed in the Zhuang and Miao Autonomous Prefecture of Wenshan. There are 11 places (12 locations), including the cliff engravings on the Dawang Cliff in the Malipo, Heiqinglong in Qiubei, Kazi in the Yanshan, Nongka in Guangnan and the Shizi Mountain in Benggu of Xichou, covering an area of approximately 5,430 square meters, with more than 170 engravings and over 400 designs. The second type is bone-carved books. The ancestors of the Zhuang Ethnic Minority in Yunnan had a long history of carving patterns on utensils, animal bones and even human body, which are still passed on and used in some areas. Among them, the most famous one is bone-carved almanac calculator in the Zhuang Ethnic Minority. The Committee of Ethnic and Religious Affairs of Zhuang and Miao Autonomous Prefecture of Wenshan discovered 58 bone carvings within its territory. Bone carvings, known as "Jiabake" and "Wajiaba" in Zhuang Language, refer to graphic symbols and books engraved on the bone pieces, which were the utensils used by the primitive people for calculating calendars and divination. Animal bones were usually engraved with figures, tables, coffins, plants, bows and arrows, animals, dry railings, sun patterns and other images, which are pictographs with both aesthetic and memory functions. The third type refers to the statues of gods. Majority of the engravings in the Zhuang Ethnic Minority are statues of gods, with diverse types and abundant works, implying the secular concept of avoiding evil by the power of "god". The aesthetic attitude and emotion are intertwined. According to its content, shapes and use, it can be roughly divided into three categories: long-scroll statues of gods in the Mo Religion, religious wall pictures and divination paintings. Among them, long-scroll statues of gods in the Mo Religion are among the unique religious images of the religion, which is inherited and used by the priests in the Mo Religion. Painted on the homespun linen, the statues are in long vertical-scroll form. Besides, column painting are made, mostly used for funeral and tomb-sweeping ceremonies.

3. Ancient Books of the Dai Ethnic Minority

The Dai Ethnic Minority has its own ethnic written language. Most of the ancient books and records in the Dai Language are carving and writing copies, manuscripts and transcripts. There are two kinds of ancient books and records, i.e., pattra-leaf and paper (tissue and vellum paper) books. The shape and structure are generally composed of the form of two plaques sandwiched together, folding and traditional thread binding, which are mainly spread in the Dai areas of Xishuangbanna, Dehong, Baoshan, Pu 'er, Lincang, Honghe and other prefectures and cities.

According to the contents, ancient books of Dai Language can be divided into the religious category such as *Lang Si She Bu Xian Zai, Prayer for Chicken Sacrifice to the Water God, Prayer for the Soul of the Rice Sacrifice*, and *The Conjuring Words*, the political and historical category such as *The Le History* and *Xuanfu History of Menglian*, the literature and art category including *Batamaga Pengshangluo, Lan Ga Xi He*, and *Li Feng*, as well as the categories of astronomy and calendar, farmland water conservancy, medicine, theory monograph, military martial arts, language and characters, translation and other categories.

Non-paper ancient book carriers of the Dai Ethnic Minority are provided with the characteristics of a variety of forms and large quantities, the most representative of which are the silverware, pattra-leaf scriptures and ancient painting books of the Dai Ethnic Minority. Among them, pattra-leaf scriptures are the most typical non-paper ancient books and records. The pattra-leaf scriptures, known as "Tanlan" in Dai Language, are carved on specially-made pattra leaves with the stencil pen (a cutting tool used in carving seals, etc.) by local people. Furthermore, wall and cloth paintings and other non-paper painting books and records are also quite distinctive.

4. Ancient Books of the Yi Ethnic Minority

The Yi Ethnic Minority has its own language and writing system. Yi Language is a category of the Yi language branch of the Tibeto-Burman Group of Sino-Tibetan Languages, divided into six big dialects of the east, west, south, north, central and southeast regions. The Yi Ethnic Minority has its own ancient writing system, which was called "Yi Scriptures" "Cuan characters", "Luoluo characters", etc. in ancient Chinese books and records. Currently, they are collectively known as "ancient Yi Language". Each character pattern represents a literal meaning, and there are various ways of writing. There are over 10,000 character forms in the existing ancient Yi character, with over 1,000 words in common use. In history, ancestors of the Yi Ethnic Minority used ancient Yi Language to write voluminous literature and books as well as numerous inscriptions, covering politics, military affairs, philosophy, religion, history, geography, language, writing system, literature, art, astronomy, calendar, medicine, health and other fields. The ancient Yi books and records popular in the Yi Ethnic Minority in modern times mainly include paper, leather, cloth, bone, cliff, wooden slips, wood engraving, inscriptions, seals and other carrier forms, of which, paper books account for an absolute proportion, including transcripts and wood-carving printed copies. There are over 20,000 volumes (pieces) of ancient books and records in Yi Language in existence, a majority of which are transcripts and minority are wood-carving printed copies. There are over 20,000 volumes (pieces) of ancient books and records in Yi Language in existence. Ancient Books and records in Yi Language in Yunnan can be divided into ancient books and records in Yi Language in South Yunnan, Luquan and Wuding, Sani, Azhe, Xuanwei, Luoping and the north. The more representative books include the traditional religious ritual ancient books such as *Wucha, Mencha, The Scripture for Guiding passage,* The *Scripture for Dragon Worship, The Scripture for Prayer to the Heaven for Rain, Lu Zi Nan Dao, Nao Si Gu, The Scripture for Recalling the Soul of the Dead,* and *Ni Bu Mu Si,* the famous literary work such as *Ashima* and *Nimi Poem,* the creation epics such as *Chamu, Axi's xianji, Meige, Ahei Xinimo,* and *Ni Su Duo Jie,* and the literature long poems in translation such as *Dong Yong and Qi Xiannü Celestial, The Phoenix, Muhe and Weiye , Tangwang's Wandering to the Other World,* and *Tang Monks' Journey for Buddhist Scriptures.*

The most representative non-paper ancient books and records of the Yi Ethnic Minority in Yunnan are cliff engravings in Yi Language. For instance, the Cliff Engraving Depicting History of the Flourishing Age of Luowu (the carved area is 206cm×80cm in height) is the long-piece inscription in Yi Language with a relatively large history and retained relatively complete in the Yi Ethnic Minority in the southwest region of China within the territory of Yi and Miao Autonomous County in Luquan of Kunming City, which was engraved in the 10th year during the reign of Emperor Jiajing of the Ming Dynasty (1531A. D.). It has a history of over 480 years, recording the prosperous history of 14 generations of Feng's hereditary headmen in Wuding in more than 350 years.

Each ethnic minority in Yunnan has or once had more or less non-paper ancient books and records. Since the establishment of the People's Republic of China, especially in the 1980s, many non-paper ancient books and records have been rescued and protected. Some are preserved in various collection institutions at all levels, some are displayed in various kinds of museums, and some have received relevant research results. Nevertheless, a great many non-paper ancient books and records, such as cliff engravings hidden in the deep mountains are exposed to the weather, have been changed a lot, or even have disappeared. For instance, bone carvings in the Zhuang Ethnic Minority were scattered here and there, and no one has interpreted them. The investigators intended to seek and discover the profound mysteries, but they failed. For another example, due to the taboo of using ritual items, wooden plaques were destroyed immediately after use, it is difficult to find the ancestors' utensils... All these are not only the existing situation faced by the non-paper books and records of ethnic minorities in Yunnan, but also the dilemma faced by the ancient records of ethnic minorities.

III

Culture is the root of the ethnic groups the spiritual home of mankind, the source of a nation's cohesion, vitality and creativity, and an important support for a strong and prosperous country. The ancient books and records of ethnic minorities are true and vivid records of the historical development process of ethnic minorities, which contain the unique spiritual values, ways of thinking and extraordinary imagination and creativity of ethnic minorities. They are the treasures of human civilization and the precious cultural heritage of China. Ancient books and records of ethnic minorities have been playing an active value orientation role and a social function of practical application in the long process of spreading and communication. The value of an excellent work of ethnic ancient books and records in the national society goes far beyond the professional scope of a discipline, representing the cognition of a nation in a certain professional field, reflecting a certain historical development stage of a nation, or even bearing and representing the social facts and historical trend of a nation. It is important historical and practical significance to strengthen the rescue and protection of ancient books and records of ethnic minorities for enriching the treasure house of Chinese culture, comprehensively understanding the development course of the Chinese nation, building a new socialist ethnic relationship of equality, solidarity, mutual assistance and harmony, and promoting the cause of ethnic unity and progress.

After the establishment of the Peoples Republic of China, under the leadership of party committees and governments at all levels, remarkable achievements have been made in the rescue, protection, translation, collation and publication of ancient books and records of ethnic minorities in Yunnan Province through unremitting efforts of several generations of relevant working personnel on ancient books and records. Based on the principle of "rescue orientation, and protection first", more than 30,000 ancient books (volumes) of written literature and over 10,000 oral ancient records of ethnic minorities have been rescued. Moreover, *Complete Works of Translations and Annotations on Ancient Books and Records of Naxi Dongba*, *Complete Works of Chinese Pattra-leaf Scriptures*, *Integration of Rare Editions of Ancient Books and Records of Ethnic Minorities in Yunnan*, *Reservation of Ancient Books and Records of Cultural Heritage of the Yi Ethnic Minority in Honghe*, *Complete Works of Classical Epics of Ethnic Minorities in Yunnan*, *Complete Works of Narrative Poems of Ethnic Minorities in Yunnan* and other representative ethnic ancient book and record achievements have attracted extensive attentions at home and abroad. However, the current achievements of the rescue, protection, translation and compilation are not worth mentioning for the voluminous ancient books and records of ethnic minorities. It is roughly estimated that in addition to the collected and preserved ancient books and records of ethnic minorities, there are still more than 70,000 ancient books (volumes) of the ethnic minority literature scattered in Yunnan. Due to numerous reasons such as improper preservation or no inheritance, it is difficult to carry out active-state inheritance for many ancient books scattered among the people. Moreover, many ancient books are lost or damaged, so the rescue and protection task is urgent. The specific regional conditions of the non-paper ancient books and records of ethnic minorities in Yunnan are especially worrying. The majority of part of the movable, non-paper ancient books with cultural relic value have been collected and preserved by the institutions at all levels, enterprises and private people. The rescue and protection work maximizes the cultural value of such ancient books and records. However, after the collection and preservation of ancient books of ethnic minorities, the national wisdom crystallization, which could have been passed down in the folk in active state, can easily become the treasure in the private book cabinets that no one else knows. There are still various kinds of people paying visits to the mountains and villages to search for the small number of ancient books and records of ethnic minorities, some of which have been resold overseas at a profit. Meanwhile, the specific regional conditions for many immovable non-paper ancient books and records are even more regrettable. These stone carvings and cliff engravings bearing ethnic culture are mostly hidden in deep mountains, which are exposed to the weather all the year round. Therefore, the writing symbols or handwriting are so blurred that it is difficult to identify them, or they have directly been damaged by human beings. Natural erosion and gradual disappearance of the stone carvings and cliff engravings is the natural law of development, but it is a huge loss for the ethnic culture.

We have experienced and witnessed several painful moments during the preparation of this series of books. With the support of Yunnan Provincial Department of Finance and Yunnan Provincial Commission of Ethnic and Religious Affairs, we have been consistently pushing forward the project of *Integration of Rare Editions of Ancient Books and Records of Ethnic Minorities in Yunnan*, which is among the one hundred excellent cultural projects in Yunnan Province. Meanwhile, according to the requirements specified in *Notification on the 13th Five-year Plan for the Protection of Ancient Books and Records of Ethnic Minorities issued by National Ethnic Affairs Commission of the People's Republic of China*, "the national census on ancient books of ethnic minorities have been basically completed; the census work has been fully promoted together with relevant departments to find out the resources of ancient books and records of ethnic minorities in various regions. Moreover, the census registration management system shall be established and improved; and a census registration platform shall be constructed to enter, calculate and summarize the census information of ancient books and records of ethnic minorities in various regions, so that the national census registration catalogue of ancient books and records of ethnic minorities can be established." In line with the purpose of "understanding the basic condition and building a platform", we have conducted a general survey and collection of ancient books and records of ethnic minorities in Yunnan Province. For this purpose, we have visited the collection institutions of ancient books and records of ethnic minorities in every prefecture and city of Yunnan Province, and paid visits to the inheritors of ancient books and records and the collectors. Our footprints have almost covered all the regions of Yunnan Province. When we conducted research in Diqing Tibetan Autonomous Prefecture in 2016, the Research Institute of Tibetan Studies in Diqing Tibetan Autonomous Prefecture introduced the preservation and distribution of non-paper ancient books and records in the prefecture, and mentioned that there were many Tibetan stone carvings on the hillside near Tacheng Town of Weixi County. We found the pictures taken by the institute during the field research in the computer several years ago. We could see that half of the hillside was covered with stone carvings, which were all age-old cultural relics. We were so excited. Since there were only a few miles between the distribution location of the stone carvings and Gezi Village where the *Grid Tablet Inscription* engraved in Tibetan language in the Tang Dynasty, and the stone carvings were hidden in the deep mountain, there may be some valuable non-paper ancient records. Unfortunately, we didn't bring the shooting equipment with us, so we decided to go there for investigation later. We didn't expect that we had missed the chance to see its elegant style and features. In May 2018, we organized professional photo-taking, transferring and rubbing personnel to visit Diqing Tibetan Autonomous Prefecture. Led by relevant comrades of Tibetan Institute of Diqing Tibetan Autonomous Prefecture, the group went through the road repair, traffic jam, and hiking in the mountains and came to the hillside tirelessly. However, the scene shocked us, there was no stone carving at all, but a mound mixed with a stone of 5~6 meters in height on the slope. A few Paris polyphylla were planted in the red earth below. After several twists and turns, we got in touch with the comrades of the village committee, and learned that the village had specially assigned bulldozers to level the land so as to develop agricultural economy, and these stone carvings were buried under the mound. This is just a trivial matter we have experienced in the process of the rescue and protection of ancient books and records of ethnic minorities in Yunnan. Such things are happening not only in Diqing, but also in all the regions all over the province. All the stone carvings, cliff engraving, paper literature, silk books, bamboo-slip and wooden engraving are all confronted with such living dilemma. Personnel devoted to the rescue and protection of the ethnic culture felt deeply distressed, but deeply understand that the force of a department and even some groups is so weak to carry out the rescue and protection task. Based on such situation, it is urgent to rescue and protect non-paper ancient books and records. In view of the restriction of funds, personnel, technology and various other aspects, it is suggested that pictures of these culture heritages should be kept for the use of social science research even using the simplest and the most traditional way. Meanwhile, we call on the whole society to attach importance to the rescue and protection of ethnic ancient books and records, which is a profound cause, and also the most actual starting point at the beginning of planning of this series of books.

Yunnan People's Publishing House has offered vigorous supports to the rescue, protection, collation and publication of ancient books and records of ethnic minorities in Yunnan. The project of the rescue and protection of non-paper ancient books and records of ethnic minorities in Yunnan Province was funded by the publication fund for ancient books and records in the ethnic minority languages through application in 2016. Several years ago, Yunnan Provincial Planning Office of Sorting and Publishing Ancient Books of Ethnic Minorities collected ancient books and records from the ethnic minority areas for many times, trying to obtain the clues and take pictures. Yunnan non-paper ancient books and records collected by Lijiang Museum, Lijiang Dongba Culture Research Institute, the Library in Yulong Naxi Autonomous County of Lijiang and Yunnan non-paper ancient books and records collected by folk collectors are finally integrated and published in this book after years of efforts. In order to collect these non-paper ancient books and records, relevant personnel have made great efforts and their footprints almost covered the whole regions of Yunnan Province. After collecting a great deal of original data, we encountered unprecedented difficulties in the classification and integration of the ancient books and records. Carriers of the non-paper ancient books and records in various ethnic minorities can be said to be in a great variety, and the quantity and quality of each carrier type of ancient books and records are at different levels. Since it is taken as the carrier form of a series of books that are summarized and published and comprehensively cover the representative non-paper ancient books and records, it should also take the non-paper ancient books and records covering all the ethnic minorities into account. Not only shall the precious and fine works of non-paper ancient books and records of various ethnic minorities be identified and selected, but also the emotional value of ethnic ancient books in ethnic society shall be taken into consideration as much as possible. The precious ancient books shall be objectively collected and included, and the volume and scale of books shall be also taken into consideration. Through several confirmations, we find that it is almost impossible to classify the non-paper ancient books and records in Yunnan in accordance with the discipline classification of the ethnic ancient books and records. We can only make a general classification of the non-paper ancient books and records that we have collected with all our efforts, and then classify each volume into different subcategories. The rescue and protection of ancient books and records of ethnic minorities is a long-term painstaking task, which cannot be completed in a short period. We were expected to present the high-quality and precious works of Yunnan non-paper ancient books and records comprehensively, but we are constantly discovering new ancient books and records and expanding new categories in our practical work. Therefore, there are inevitably some improper aspects in the series of books, so we can only hope for the forgiveness and corrections of the experts earnestly.

In conclusion, this series of books are the first large-scale integration and collection of non-paper ancient books and records of ethnic minorities in Yunnan. It is for the first time that numerous ancient books and precious records of ethnic minorities, which have been kept secret in the past, are shown to the public. They have been provided with many unique features in terms of academic, historical, inheritance, appreciation and collection value. Moreover, it is of great significance in protecting the cultural heritage of various ethnic minorities, carrying forward their excellent culture, enhancing ethnic unity and promoting the construction of the common spiritual homeland of the Chinese Ethnic Peoples.

目录

云南少数民族非纸质典籍聚珍

YUNNAN SHAOSHU MINZU FEIZHIZHI DIANJI JUZHEN

YUNNAN SHAOSHU MINZU
FEIZHIZHI DIANJI JUZHEN

云南少数民族非纸质典籍聚珍

傣族银刻

傣族拥有自己的民族文字，使用西双版纳傣文（傣泐文）、德宏傣文（傣纳文）、勐定傣文（傣绷文）、金平傣文（傣端文）四种拼音文字。

傣文古籍内容丰富，涉及政治、哲学、法律、历史、宗教、军事、文学、艺术、语言、文字、地理、天文、历算、经济、医药、生产生活等领域，主要流传于西双版纳、德宏、保山、普洱、临沧、红河等州市傣族聚居区。现存傣泐文古籍储量最多，其次是傣纳文古籍，傣绷文、傣端文古籍储量较少。傣文古籍多为刻本、写本、稿本和抄本，载体材料主要有贝叶、绵纸、金石器物等，其中非纸质典籍贝叶经储量丰富、最具民族特色。相比之下，傣族的金石载体古籍留存较少，但极具特色。

使用银片来记事是傣族的传统记事方法，人们常常在银片上用傣文或巴利文来记录下发生的重大事件。傣文银刻留存较少，但具有重要的文物价值和研究价值。在傣族传统文化中，只有一些弥足珍贵的、需要长期保留的内容才会用傣文记载在金属器物上。这些记录着重要信息的银片，以银作为载体，以贝叶为形制，内容主要涉及南传上座部佛教及傣族地区土司承袭或重大事件的相关文书。无论是出土的塔铭，还是传世的南传佛教上座部升阶记事银片，都具有极高的史料价值，大部分被收藏在各地博物馆及相关机构中，难得一见。这些铭刻类古籍对于人们探寻南传佛教上座部世界在中国的传播痕迹、传入时间、僧阶制度与当地文化的整合等方面，有着重要意义。

傣族银刻主要有塔铭和南传上座部佛教僧侣升阶档案两类。西双版纳佛塔建立之初，为了恭迎佛法、供奉佛陀的遗物，人们将塔视为佛陀的化身；建塔时，塔心必置一金板或银板，上刻建塔年月和经咒，同时也把一些金、银、琉璃、金属货币珍藏于塔内。这些刻录了文字的塔铭，对于了解当时南传上座部佛教的历史有着重要意义。

南传上座部佛教的僧阶制度根据僧人的年龄、洼节、学行，按照一定标准对僧侣进行层级划分。僧阶是僧团内部以及世俗社会对于僧侣佛学修养、持戒修行的共同认可，僧阶层级及其划分标准、晋升仪式等共同构成僧阶制度。西双版纳地区的南传上座部佛教在漫长的传播过程中形成了较为成熟的僧阶制度，在僧阶层级、晋升仪式和晋升条件上有着严格的规定。民国时期，西双版纳地区的润派根据年龄、洼节、学行划分为十级僧阶（也有八僧阶说）：一帕诺，二帕，三都，四都龙，五祜巴，六帕召祜，七沙弥，八僧伽罗阁，九松列，十松列·阿嘎牟尼。因此，目前留存的升阶档案以西双版纳地区的为主。

云南省博物馆收藏的南传上座部佛教僧侣升阶档案十分完整，极其珍贵，均为贝叶经形制的银片錾刻傣文而成。该档案以西双版纳总佛寺大长老松列·阿嘎牟尼的升阶记事银片为主，一共6页，涵盖了都比、祜巴、玛萨米、桑卡拉扎、松列、松列 · 阿嘎牟尼等主要僧阶的升阶步骤。这批升阶记事银片记载了其佛学生涯中的每一个重要时刻，真实记录了民国时期南传上座部佛教的僧阶制度面貌，反映了一些重大历史事件。通过对这些记事银片的解读，我们得以对南传佛教僧阶制度有了更生动、具体的认识。

尽管有文字记录，但对记事银片铭文内容的解读，仍然存在种种困难。铭文涉及文字众多，多为傣泐文、巴利文，部分为泰文、缅文、老挝文，时间跨度长、翻译难度大，在对铭文进行解读与翻译中，不仅要求有极高的语言能力，还要对地区历史、民族文化及南传上座部佛教有一定程度的了解。从目前收集的信息来看，使用银片来记录档案及重要事件是可信的，然而银片上的文字也有可能“不是初建的原始记载，而是后来某个时期翻修或重建时根据人们的口传而记录藏进去的”。因此，我们既要充分利用、肯定其第一手资料的价值，又要通过对文本文献或其他参照物展开解读，从而对其史料价值加以判断与认知。

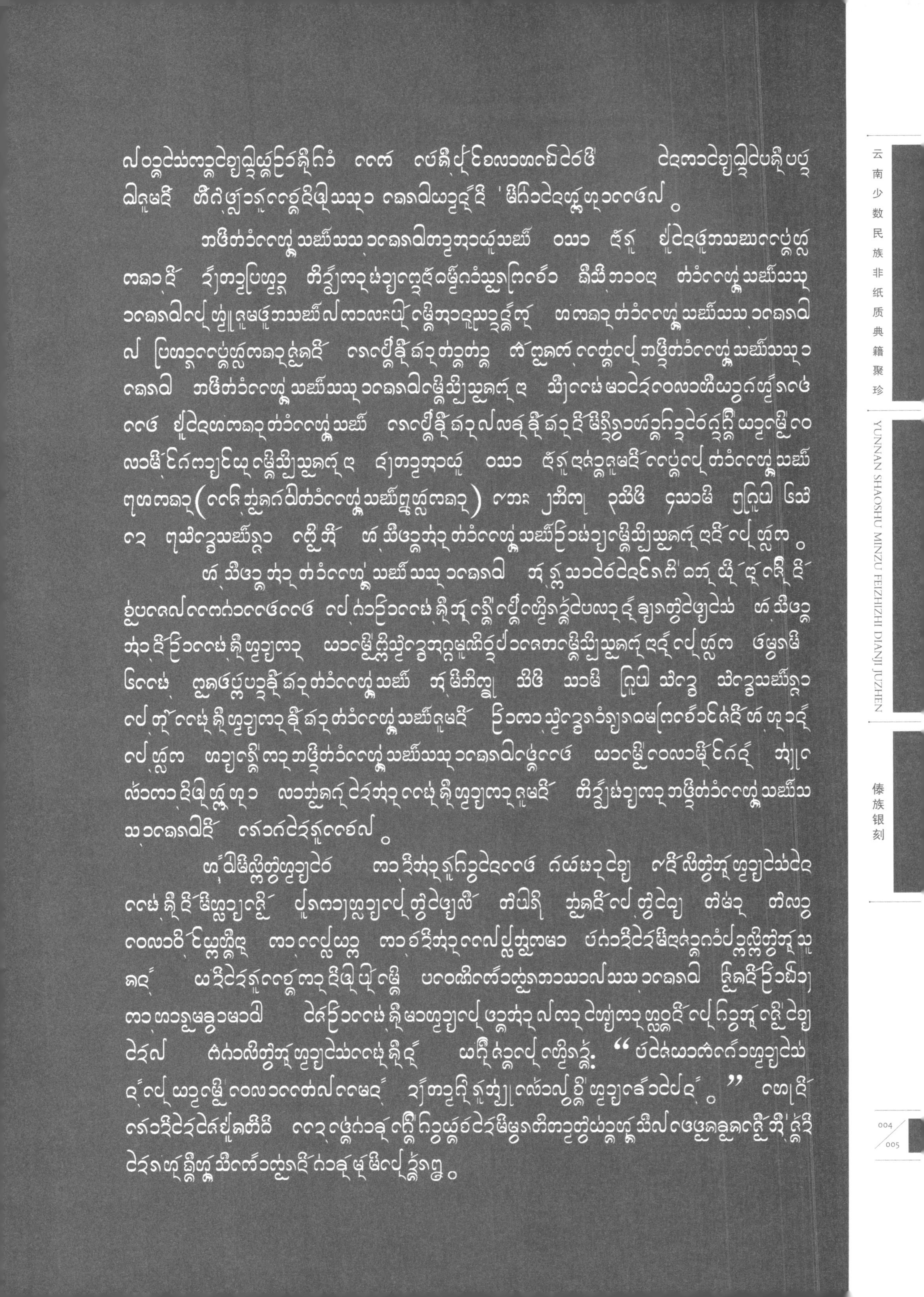

[illegible]

请旋转图书阅读

松列·阿嘎牟尼在西双版纳总佛寺晋升为都比记事银片
年代：傣历 1285 年
收藏单位：云南省博物馆

松列·阿嘎牟尼从都比升为玛哈厅（祜巴）记事银片
年代：傣历 1298 年 7 月 15 日
收藏单位：云南省博物馆

请旋转图书阅读

总领全勐佛寺的至尊祜巴英达、总管议事庭的尊敬的松列摩诃儒瓦拉、总管宫廷外事的尊敬的摩诃拉扎沙塔及西双版纳各勐召勐，恭迎祜巴西利彭（尖达彭）晋升为玛萨米西利彭记事银片

年代：傣历 1298 年

收藏单位：云南省博物馆

松列·阿嘎牟尼在佛教协会、僧众和信众的见证下，从祜巴升为桑卡拉扎记事银片

年代：傣历 1318 年 1 月 2 日

收藏单位：云南省博物馆

松列·阿嘎牟尼在佛教协会、僧众和信众的见证下，从桑卡拉扎升为松列记事银片
年代：傣历 1318 年 1 月 2 日
收藏单位：云南省博物馆

松列·阿嘎牟尼在佛教协会、僧众和信众的见证下，从松列升为松列·阿嘎牟尼记事银片
年代：傣历 1318 年 1 月 2 日
收藏单位：云南省博物馆

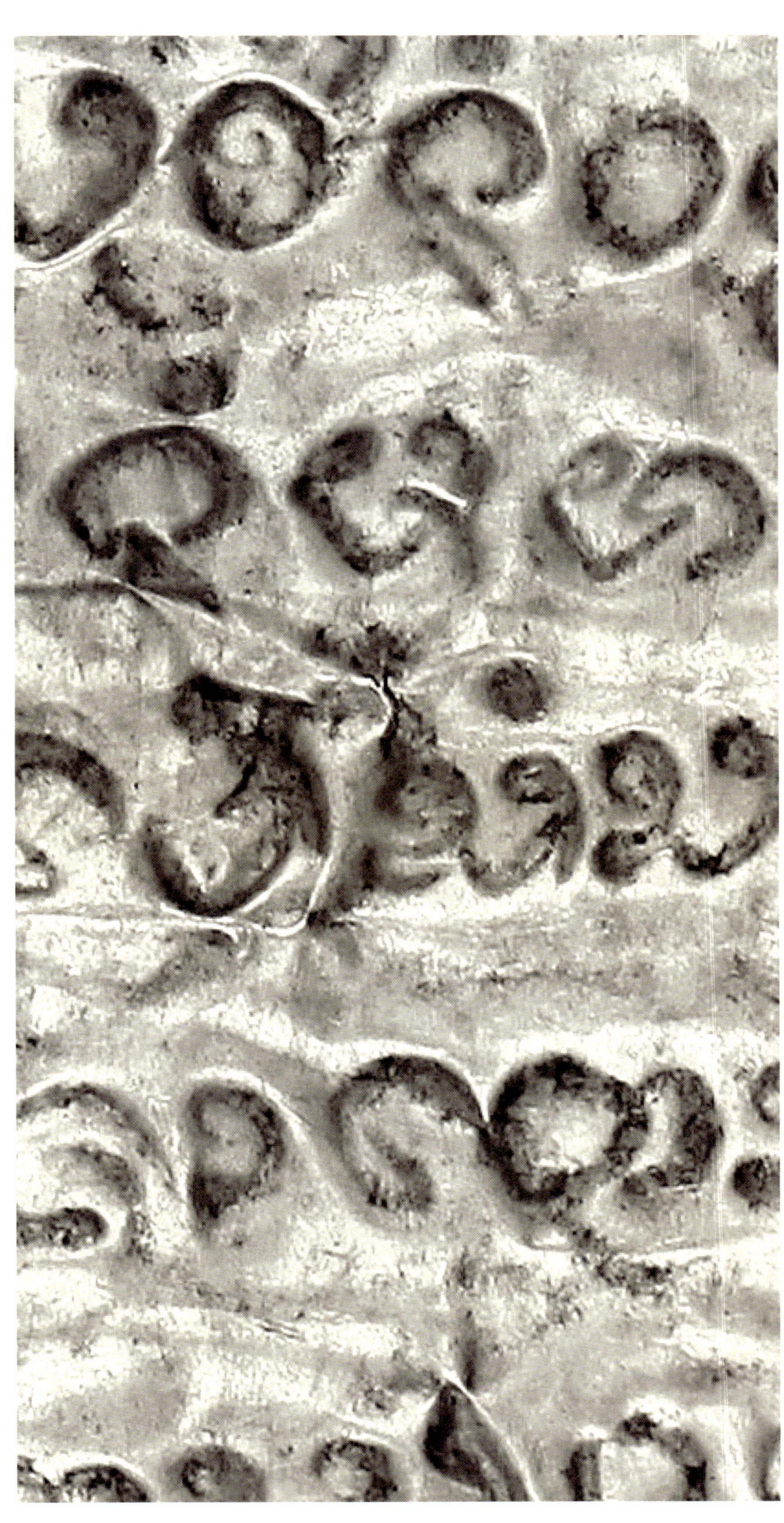

傣文塔铭
年代：清代
收藏单位：西双版纳傣族自治州勐海县文化馆

请旋转图书阅读

勐罕土司委任状记事银片

年代：清代

收藏单位：云南省博物馆

勐罕土司委任状记事银片（局部）

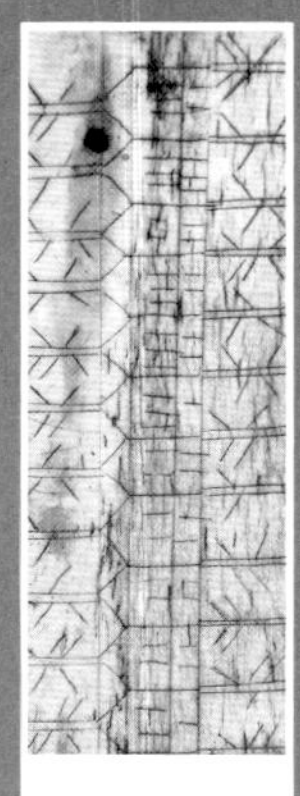

YUNNAN SHAOSHU MINZU FEIZHIZHI DIANJI JUZHEN

云南少数民族非纸质典籍聚珍

壮族骨刻书

壮族骨刻书，又称骨刻历算与预测器。壮族信奉原始的摩教，崇拜祖先，崇尚自然。远古时候的壮族先民遇到未知之事都要去求教布洛陀（大王之祖）。布洛陀便教布摩用签卦占卜自寻答案。至今，壮族民众凡遇大事、难事，布摩仍会用签卦占卜。因此相信占卜的壮族民间有大量的卜辞和历算预测器传世，成为壮族民间流传最久、最具民族特征的非纸质典籍。

相传，骨刻书是母系氏族社会的“乜閏”（女皇、女王）观天象发现 15 天有月亮，15 天看不到月亮，周而复始，于是便定 30 天为一个月，12 个月为一年，并将其观察发现记录下来。经过数千年的传承和发展，壮族骨刻书不断完善定型。

壮族布摩使用的骨刻书，戴光禄、何正廷在《壮族文化概论》一书中做了深入、客观的研究，认为：骨刻历算器，壮语叫“甲巴克”。“甲”，壮语“片”的意思，“巴克”为“刻度”。用水牛肋骨片做的叫“甲长歪”，用黄牛肋骨片做的叫“甲长莫”，统称“甲巴克”。其上有 30 个刻度（壮语叫“巴克稳亨”），正反两面合用，计有 60 卡，为干支计日的一个周期，可以推算出 60 甲子中任何一日应在的刻度。并结合月亮圆缺望朔情况，依据摩经关于“初三生月芽 / 十五月亮明 / 二七月入睡 / 三十月最暗”的记述，正月启寅，从第一缺数起，二月启卯，从第二缺数起，依此类推，逐月逐日推算，即可得出简单年历。骨刻书上还刻有表示农事、房屋、鸡卦三层内容各异的图纹符号，由布摩用以预测吉凶，曾兼行物候历。简言之，“甲巴克”即是通过观察太阳运行、月亮圆缺望朔、候鸟来去及植物荣枯的内在联系和变化规律，掌握物候历算方法，以指导耕耘、播种、收获等。

壮族历史传说提及祖先曾使用过一种叫“司莱”的文字，壮语意思即图画文字。而在一般的壮语中，写作“莱司”或“猎司”，“莱司”含义与“司莱”一致，“猎司”的“猎”汉语是“画”的意思。壮族人民把写字说成是“画字”，说明了壮族的文字与“图画”有一定的关系，也说明壮族先民在发明方块壮字前，曾用图画来记事并表达各种意思和愿望。故而，何正廷在《句町国史》一书中指出：历算器上除了刻有鸡卜卦象之外，还有表示农事栽种、起房盖屋等诸多内容各异的图纹符号，这种图符具有以形表意的功能，虽然还没有标音的功能，但是已经成为标识语言的“引导字”或“引导词”，更有记事、标识、提示、凭借、艺术等功能。

壮族骨刻书是壮族原始宗教信仰的产物，也是反映壮族历史文化的实物遗存。因其产生的历史较为久远，对其产生的历史、文化内涵等研究有待进一步深入。我们将其收录并整理出版，是为了将骨刻书这一真实反映壮族先民农业生产和社会生活的实物载体作为非纸质古籍去抢救保护，也为了解壮族历史文化特别是农耕文化提供实物资料。

Sw jiabmbaek bouxcuengh,goj ruangx aen naeb'anq jiabmbaek daj naeb zwz.Bouxcuengh sinq hoek yengh mo zohnduq laehmaz haenj,gih mbod buqyah,jingh nengz bonaemx.Liuz hax,zwznduq ndowjnanz goenz bouxcuengh zohnduq nahgah mex hoj saeh gaeng mboqrux gaz bae vanz cham buqloegdoz(Buqyah lauxhongz).Buqloegdoz zoq suan pujmo ywj nduk haeg naeb. Taeng gaunaeh,goenz bouxcuengh nah mex saeh dwx、saeh raix,pujmo goj nwngz ywj nduk naeb saeh.Baenzvenj,ndaw mbanj bouxcuengh miz gaemz naeb daj aen naeb liux loengz lai,baenz zawh yengh zohnduq mboq aeu sa laeh maz liuz ndaej ndowj nyiuz、naux haeg miz yaiz pujzoeg nyiuz haenj.

Liuz hax,sw jiabmbaek zawh"Mehhongz"mbongj pujnyingz dang zaeuj haenj ngaeux aenfax taen siphaj ngoenz miz hai,siphaj ngoenz ngangh mboqtaen hai,hoekvenj laihlwh. Baenzvenj zoq dingh samsip ngoenz baenz ndon lux,sipngih ndon baenz bi lux,nwngz laiz dix ngaeux taen haenj loengzdaeuj.Zoh laeng dauh ked rangh"Mehhongz"yuq ndaw sw jiabmbaek. Laeh gaq jiq tiang bi laehdaeb daj raenghkwnj,sw jiabmbaek bouxcuengh gahraeng gah hoek koeb dingh hunq.

Sw jiabmbaek pujmo bouxcuengh aeu taeng haenj,Daiq Guangzluh、Hoh Zwnqtinh yuq ndaw buk sw《Tuam hax Vwnhhuaq bouxcuengh》nduanj hoek ndaej ndaek、hiamhoj yaj,hax zawh:Aen jiabmbaek naeb'anq,kauq noengz ruangx"Jiabmbaek"（"Jiab", kauq noengz zoqzawh"Kaix nex", "Mbaek"zoqzawh"Mbaekmai"）.Aeu nduk changj vaiz hoek haenj ruangx"Jiab changj vaiz",aeu nduk changj moz hoek haenj ruangx"Jiab changj moz",tuam ruangx hoek"Jiabmbaek".Now dix miz samsip mbaek（Kauq noengz ruangx"Mbaek vaenzhwnz"） ,daengz song faeg zaemh tw,daengzle miz choeksip mbaek,dang zawh baez mai koeb ngoenzhunz lux,naeb oeg ndaw choeksip gaeb ngoenz rawz gojndaej zawh yuq mbaek rawz.Nwngz dungzvaed aenhai maenz vauh choaet siphaj baenzrawq,yi swmo hax"Chosam hai oeg ngaed/siphaj aenhai rungh/ngihjiat hai nezlaep/samsip hai laep nyiuz"haenj,ndonjeng aj ngiz,loh mbaek daih'aet anq maz,ndonngih aj maeuj,loh mbaek daihngih anq maz,hoekvenj laeh loengzbae,hoekndon hoekngoenz naeb,zoq ndaej oeg ngoenzhunz bi lux yaj.Now sw jiabmbaek nwngz ked miz tamai hax zawh hoekgaengx、aenronz、ywj ndukzaeq sam laeb yengh hax mboq dungzlumj haenj tiam,hawj pujmo aeu maz naeb ndae ndoeg,saenz ndaej dang hoek zawh ywj ndinfax.Hax nauxnuaix,"Jiabmbaek"zoqzawh loh ngaeux tavaenz hoekrawz daeq、aenhai maenz vauh choaet siphaj baenzrawq、dijnoeg baedauh daj go zaeu jinh choj ndaw dix dungzrangh baenzrawq daj hoekrawz bej ndaej miz ruaizlaeh gaeng yaq,ruxndeq hoekrawz naeb gahyengh ndinfax,maz yaix hoek tw ndai、sauq faenz、caeu kaeuj lenaeh.

Kauq liuz zohnduq bouxcuengh hax taeng buqyah saenz ndaej aeu yengh tasw ruangx"Swlaiz"haenj lux,kauq noengz zoqzawh ruangx sw laizva.Maj mwhndai kauq noengz hax,laizsw ruangx hoek"Laizsw"maj"Lezsw","Laizsw"hax daj"Swlaiz"baenzndiu,ta"Lez"ndaw "Lezsw"kauq haeg zawh"Va".Goenz bouxcuengh ruangx"Laizsw"zawh"Vasw",hax singj tasw bouxcuengh daj"Laizva"dungzrangh taeng,goj hax singj goenz bouxcuengh zohnduq hoek oeg swndip doekguanq,saenz ndaej aeu laizva maz nyen saeh nwngz aeu hax gahyengh zaw nwh daj yengh nguangz.Baenzvenj,Hoh Zwnqtinh yuq ndaw buk sw《Hax mowngz gaeuj ndiang》hax oeg:Now aen noeb'anq ked miz ywj ndukzaeq yaq,nwngz miz hunq mai hax najgaengx ndaem kaeuj、daengj ronz hoek ronz le yengh hax mboq dungzlumj naeh,sownh hunq mai naeh hoek baenz aeu hunq hax saeh ndaej,nwngz mboq hoek baenz mai hiang ndaej mboqguanj,gazhax baenz zawh"Tasw lingz yaix"maj"Gaemzsw lingz yaix"mai hax gaemzkauq haenj yaj,nauxzawh nwngz hoek baenz nyen saeh、mai hoek、liamhdoq、yengh dex、Yiqsuh lenaeh ndaej.

Sw jiabmbaek bouxcuengh zawh yengh bouxcuengh sinq hoek Zungzjiauq liux loengz naeuj,gojzawh yengh liux loengz ta taen hax oeg laeh gaq Vwnhhuaq bouxcuengh haenj.Cho dix oeg miz ndaej ndowj zawz,dix hoekrawz oeg miz、zawh hax taeng gaeng lenaeh nwngz taj kamj yamq lux kaeuj ndaek nduanj hoek.Gaiqraeuz caeu dix maz nwngz zang ndae oeg baenz sw,zawh cho aeu sw jiabmbaek hax oeg najgaengx raehnaz daj ngoenzhunz naemxmowngz goenz bouxcuengh zohnduq zaeh naeh dang zawh yengh zohnduq liux loengz mboq aeu sa laiz haenj bae jiuq ndaej bauj ndae,goj cho ruxndeq bouxcuengh hoekrawz laeh gaq nauxzawh sownh hax ndaem raehnaz haenj aeu oeg yengh liux miz ta taen.

文山壮族骨刻书（一）
流传地：云南省文山壮族苗族自治州

文山壮族骨刻书（二）
流传地：云南省文山壮族苗族自治州

文山壮族骨刻书（三）
流传地：云南省文山壮族苗族自治州

文山壮族骨刻书（四）
流传地：云南省文山壮族苗族自治州

文山壮族骨刻书（五）
流传地：云南省文山壮族苗族自治州

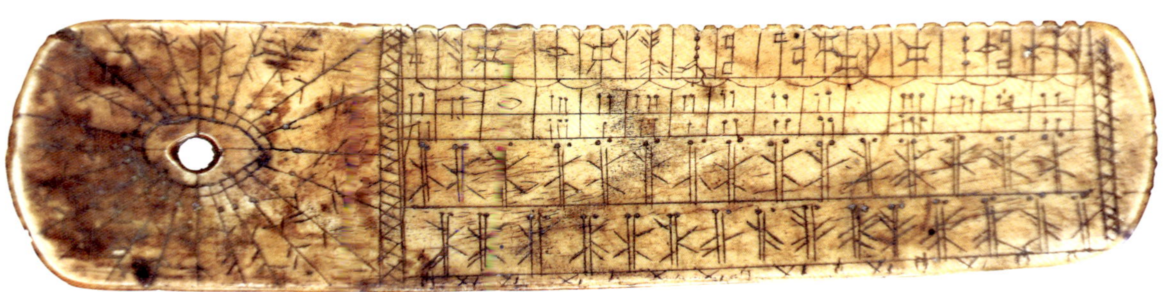

文山壮族骨刻书（六）
流传地：云南省文山壮族苗族自治州

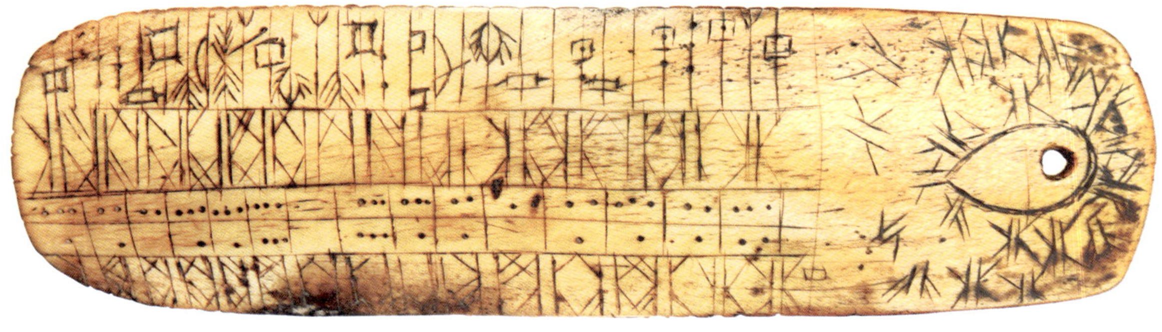

文山壮族骨刻书（七）
流传地：云南省文山壮族苗族自治州

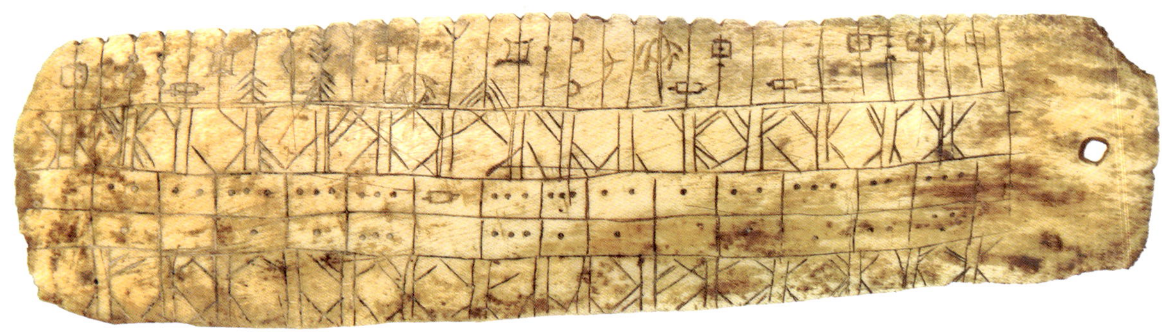

文山壮族骨刻书（八）
流传地：云南省文山壮族苗族自治州

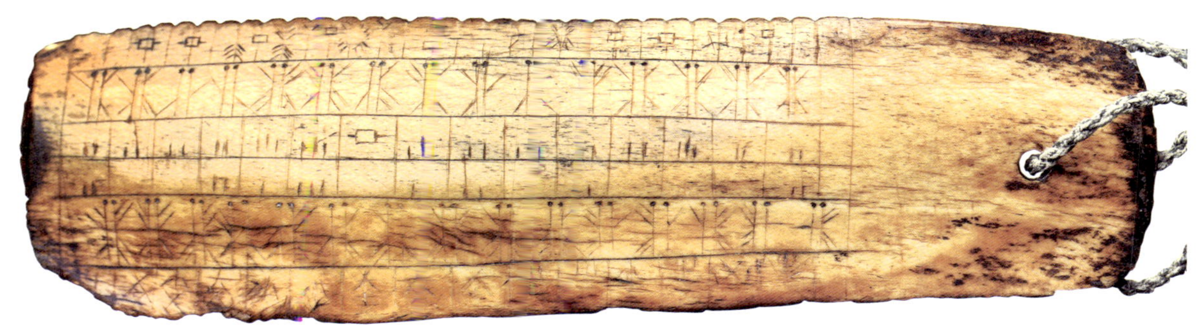

文山壮族骨刻书（九）
流传地：云南省文山壮族苗族自治州

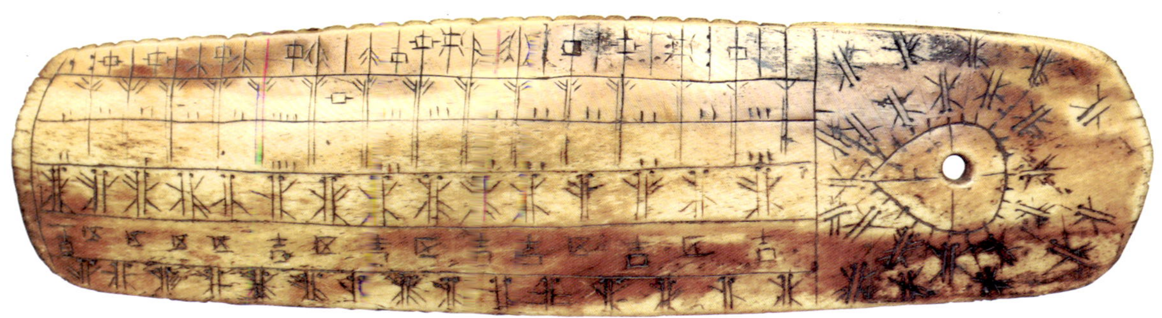

文山壮族骨刻书（十）
流传地：云南省文山壮族苗族自治州

文山壮族骨刻书（十一）
流传地：云南省文山壮族苗族自治州

文山壮族骨刻书（十二）
流传地：云南省文山壮族苗族自治州

文山壮族骨刻书（十三）
流传地：云南省文山壮族苗族自治州

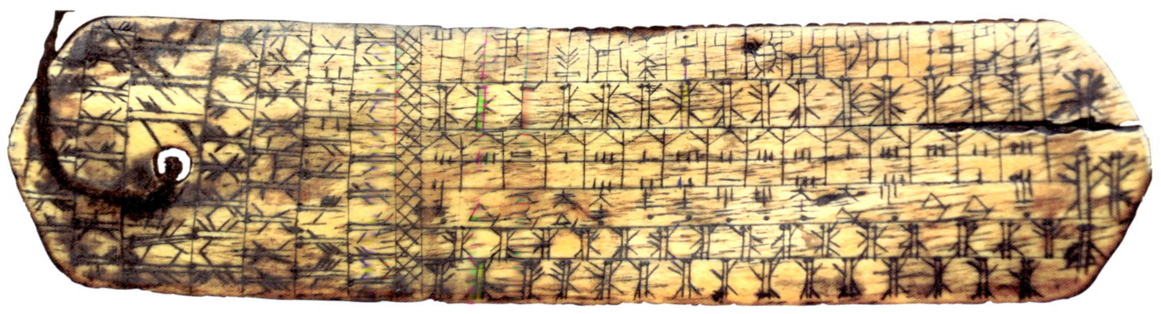

文山壮族骨刻书（十四）
流传地：云南省文山壮族苗族自治州

文山壮族骨刻书（十五）
流传地：云南省文山壮族苗族自治州

文山壮族骨刻书（十六）
流传地：云南省文山壮族苗族自治州

文山壮族骨刻书（十七）
流传地：云南省文山壮族苗族自治州

文山壮族骨刻书（十八）
流传地：云南省文山壮族苗族自治州

文山壮族骨刻书（十九）
流传地：云南省文山壮族苗族自治州

文山壮族骨刻书（二十）
流传地：云南省文山壮族苗族自治州

文山壮族骨刻书（二十一）
流传地：云南省文山壮族苗族自治州

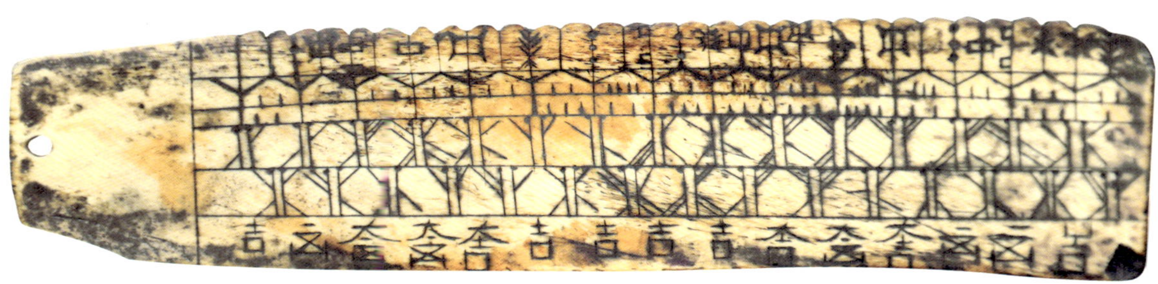

文山壮族骨刻书（二十二）
流传地：云南省文山壮族苗族自治州

文山壮族骨刻书（二十三）
流传地：云南省文山壮族苗族自治州

文山壮族骨刻书（二十四）
流传地：云南省文山壮族苗族自治州

文山壮族骨刻书（二十五）
流传地：云南省文山壮族苗族自治州

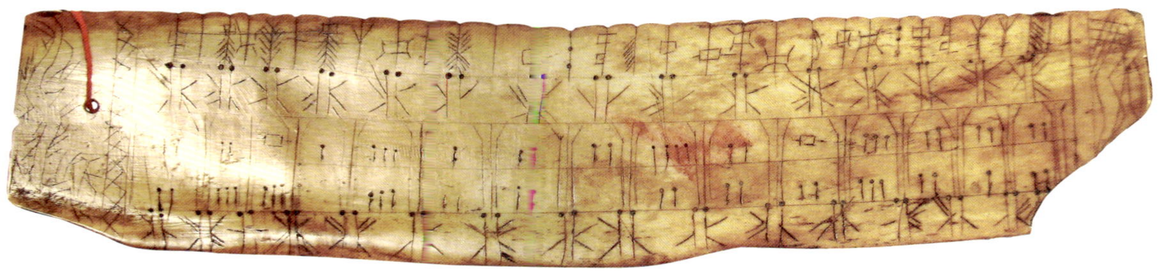

文山壮族骨刻书（二十六）
流传地：云南省文山壮族苗族自治州

文山壮族骨刻书（二十七）
流传地：云南省文山壮族苗族自治州

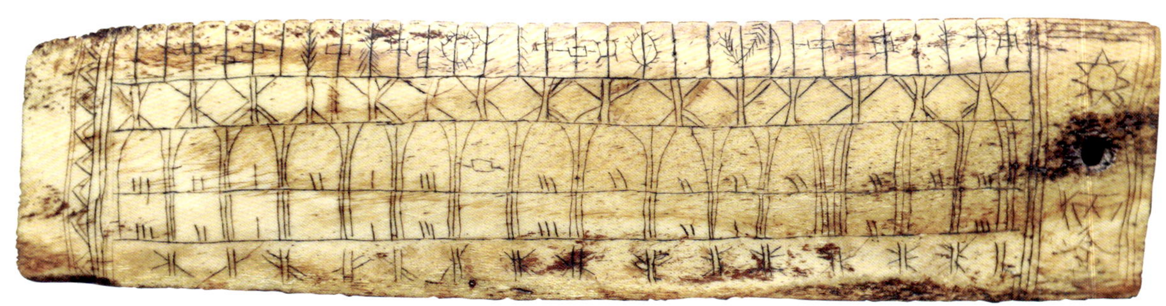

文山壮族骨刻书（二十八）
流传地：云南省文山壮族苗族自治州

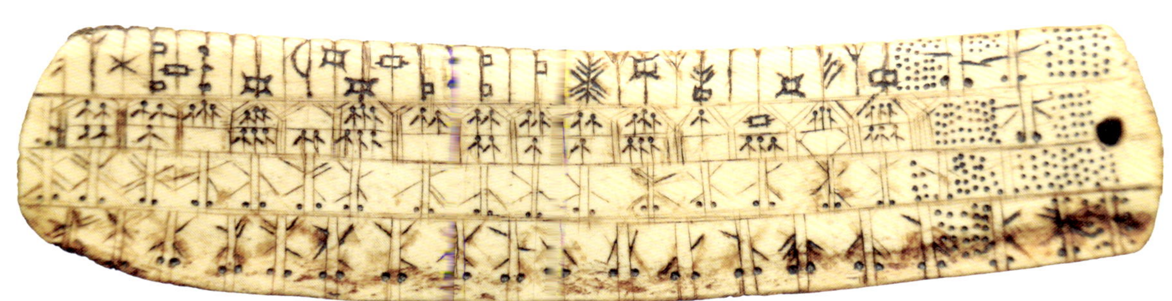

文山壮族骨刻书（二十九）
流传地：云南省文山壮族苗族自治州

文山壮族骨刻书（三十）
流传地：云南省文山壮族苗族自治州

文山壮族骨刻书（三十一）
流传地：云南省文山壮族苗族自治州

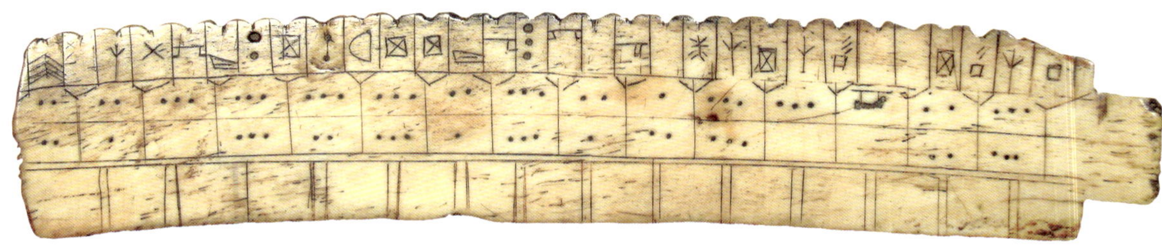

文山壮族骨刻书（三十二）
流传地：云南省文山壮族苗族自治州

文山壮族骨刻书（三十三）
流传地：云南省文山壮族苗族自治州

文山壮族骨刻书（三十四）
流传地：云南省文山壮族苗族自治州

文山壮族骨刻书（三十五）
流传地：云南省文山壮族苗族自治州

文山壮族骨刻书（三十六）
流传地：云南省文山壮族苗族自治州

文山壮族骨刻书（三十七）
流传地：云南省文山壮族苗族自治州

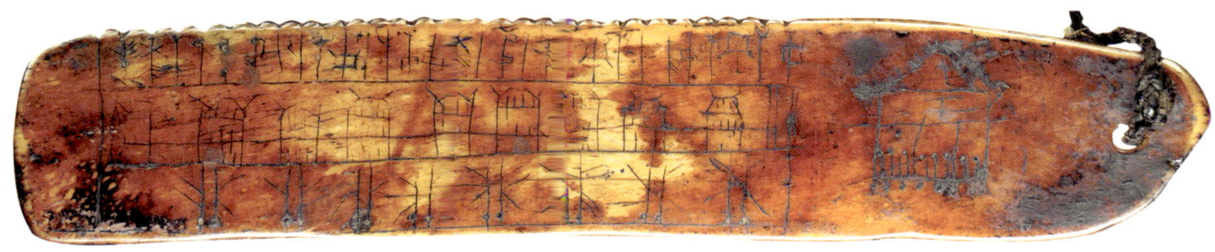

文山壮族骨刻书（三十八）
流传地：云南省文山壮族苗族自治州

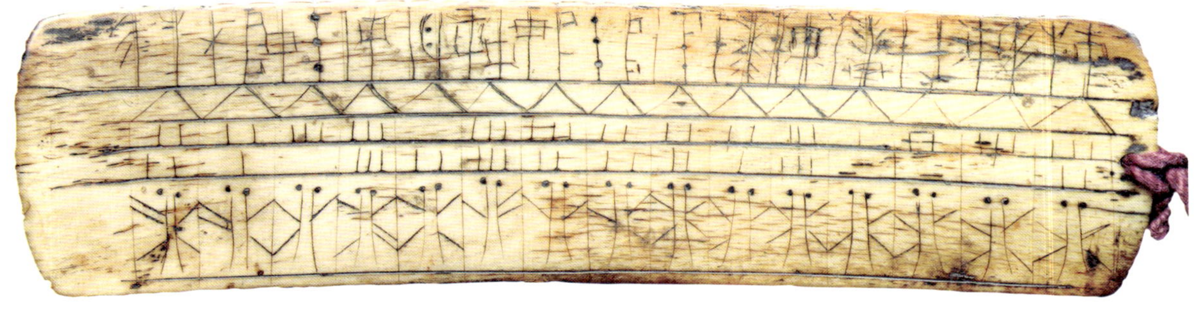

文山壮族骨刻书（三十九）
流传地：云南省文山壮族苗族自治州

文山壮族骨刻书（四十）
流传地：云南省文山壮族苗族自治州

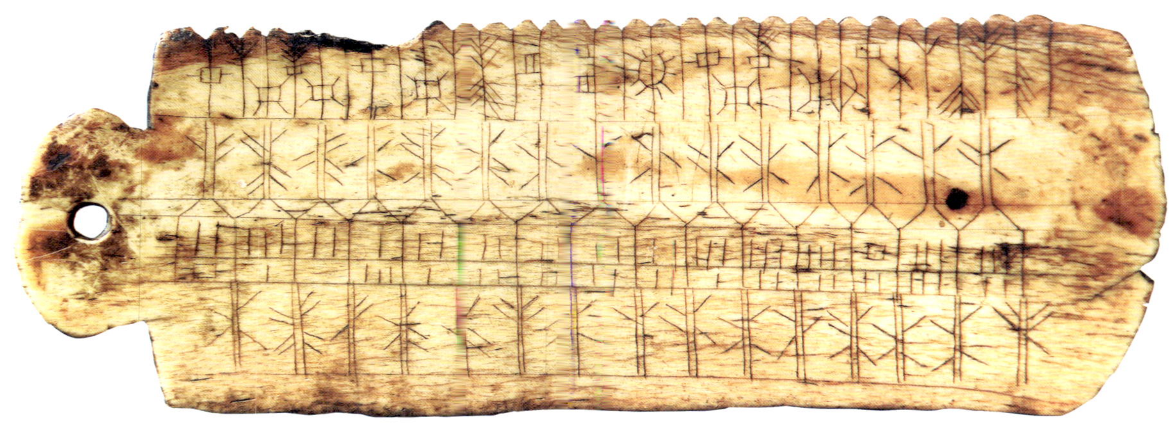

文山壮族骨刻书（四十一）
流传地：云南省文山壮族苗族自治州

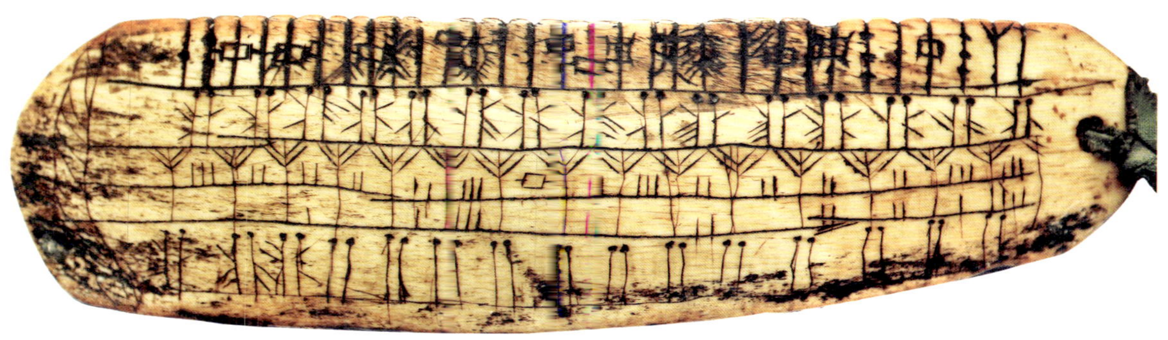

文山壮族骨刻书（四十二）
流传地：云南省文山壮族苗族自治州

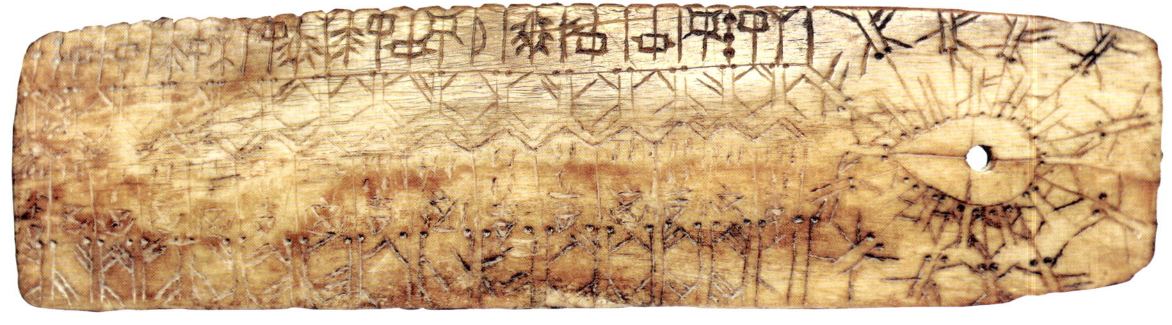

文山壮族骨刻书（四十三）
流传地：云南省文山壮族苗族自治州

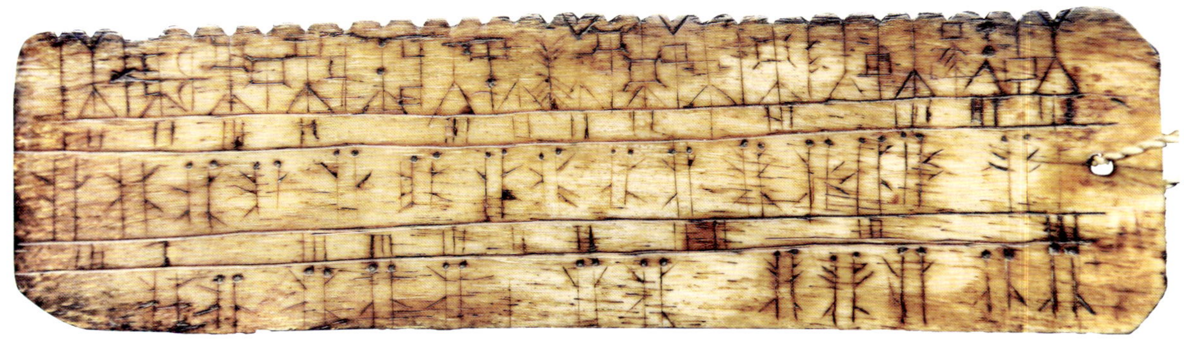

文山壮族骨刻书（四十四）
流传地：云南省文山壮族苗族自治州

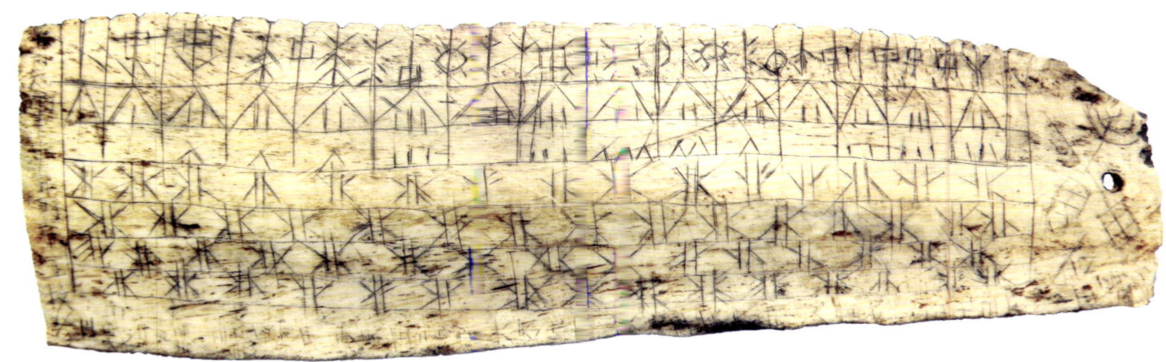

文山壮族骨刻书（四十五）
流传地：云南省文山壮族苗族自治州

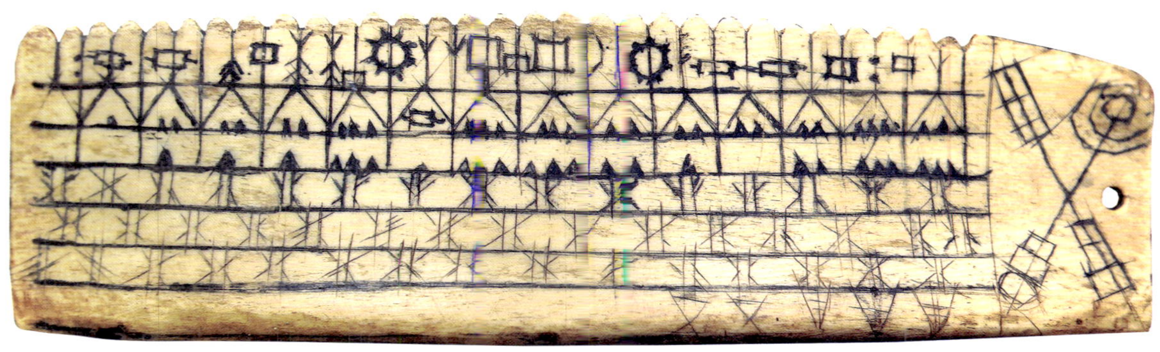

文山壮族骨刻书（四十六）
流传地：云南省文山壮族苗族自治州

文山壮族骨刻书（四十七）
流传地：云南省文山壮族苗族自治州

文山壮族骨刻书（四十八）
流传地：云南省文山壮族苗族自治州

文山壮族骨刻书（四十九）
流传地：云南省文山壮族苗族自治州

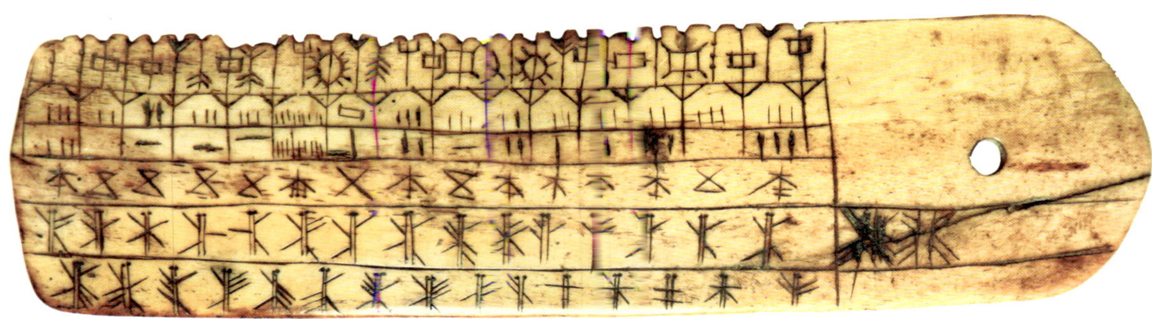

文山壮族骨刻书（五十）
流传地：云南省文山壮族苗族自治州

文山壮族骨刻书（五十一）
流传地：云南省文山壮族苗族自治州

文山壮族骨刻书（五十二）
流传地：云南省文山壮族苗族自治州

文山壮族骨刻书（五十三）
流传地：云南省文山壮族苗族自治州

文山壮族骨刻书（五十四）
流传地：云南省文山壮族苗族自治州

YUNNAN SHAOSHU MINZU FEIZHIZHI DIANJI JUZHEN

云南少数民族非纸质典籍聚珍

文山岩画

岩画，即刻画在山洞洞壁上或山崖上的图画。云南岩画自 1957 年至今已发现 60 余处，分布在怒江、澜沧江、金沙江、南盘江和红河流域。可大致分为三大区域：北部区域，沿金沙江一路向西，涉及昭通、丽江、香格里拉等地区；中部区域有昆明市石林彝族自治县、红河哈尼族彝族自治州弥勒市、玉溪市元江县等；南部区域以文山壮族苗族自治州（以下简称文山）、临沧市属的南部几个县为主。云南岩画有画面积达 1400 平方米以上，可辨图像 2400 多个，可释图形大概有人物、器物、房屋、动物、神祇和神话人物、自然物、符号和手印七类。云南岩画形式多以颜料涂绘为主，有单色涂绘、复色涂绘。画法有单色影绘（沧源岩画）、复色描画（麻栗坡大王崖岩画主体图像）、单色勾线（丘北狮子山主体图案）等；也有昆明宜良、昭通绥江等少量阴刻崖石刻凿等。

文山境内主要有南盘江—珠江和红河两大水系，沿流域分布有氐羌、百越、百濮、苗—盘瓠等诸族群，族系众多，文化多样并在长期历史发展过程中不断分化融合，创造、积淀下了各具特色的多元文化。加之州内大小山脉纵横，地貌特征多样，形成了典型的喀斯特地貌。在这些天然生成的、各族先民赖以遮风避雨、谋求生存的重要场所——山崖、石壁和洞穴，原始文字、艺术和崇拜也在这里萌芽、发生。

文山境内共有岩画点 15 个，占地约 5430 平方米，有图形 1700 余个。以写实为主，以太阳、月亮、水、人、动物等客观自然物象或动植物图像为主，亦有祭祀、骑射、劳作等描绘原始先民生活场景的图像。这些分散隐匿在大山深处、悬崖峭壁之间的未知图案又被玄妙的神话传说和祭祀活动蒙上一层神秘的色彩。有研究认为，文山岩画约产生于新石器时代至晚期铁器时代。据现有考古资料，我们可知在今壮族分布区有众多的原始刻绘艺术遗存，虽难于明确界定这些考古遗存的族属，但壮族先民是这些绘画遗存的创作者、拥有者之一是确信无疑的。

文山岩画有单色、双色和三色，以单色红色居多。用血红色和赭铁石粉绘制的崖壁画，是文山地区所有岩画的共同点。岩画物象众多，场面恢弘，人物、动物形象刻绘生动传神。先民们通过自身体验和对自然现象的观察以及综合想象，利用简单的线条、图像、符号等具体、抽象的图形或图像组合，直观真实地反映了当时自然、社会环境和人类的生产生活，也表达了他们自我创造的形式。岩画中甚至还出现了试图通过礼仪、祭祀等祈求祖先保佑、消除灾难的愿望。

“岩画是描绘在崖石上的史书”，换句话说，也是承载于非纸质载体的古籍，通过“不自觉的艺术方式”，摹写和表现先民眼中的世界，将感知映像和想象进行最初的融合，反映人类早期思维发展和世纪初创世界观的文化载体。通过一幅幅由先民们用赤铁矿粉混合着动植物分泌物创作的岩画，以表现对生活灵动的艺术辨析、临摹和解读，我们可以看到先民的物质生活和社会环境，更能知晓这些凝聚着民族感情的图画传递的信息及表达的愿望图景，并据此了解历史时期云南各族群的分布、迁徙流动和社会文化等情况。希望通过本书的介绍，让我们在领略这些刻绘在崖石、石壁上的艺术创作的至美至真的同时，也感受到它作为各民族历史遗存的深邃厚重。

Pya'ndiang,zoqzawh laizva ked daz yuq bong ngomz maj now ndanq haenj.Pya'ndiang Vinhnanh loh tiang gaeuj laeng hajsip jiet bi taeng gaunaeh taen miz choeksip lai dih yaj,ngaeuxrangh baiz yuq dah Nuqjengz、dah Lanqchangzjengz、dah Nanhpanhjengz、daj sai dah Hunghhoh,ngaeuxrangh baen baenz sam mowngz:Mowngz fang now,laeh dah Jinzcazjengz bae doq fang tavaenz doek,rangh hoj Zauztungz、Liqjengz、Cengzgowhlixlaz le mowngz naeh;Mowngz dinhzang miz Kunzminh Swq Swhlinh Cenq pujmowng haeg guanj haenj、Mihlowh Cenq Hunghhoh Zaeuz puj Haznih pujmowng haeg guanj haenj、Viqciz Swq Venhjengz Cenq lenaeh;Mowngz fang dawj miz Vwnhcanz Zaeuz bouxcuengz pujmyaux haeg guanj haenj(dawj naex daet ruangx Vwnhcanz)、jiq aen Cenq fang dawj Linhchangz Swq guanj haenj.Pya'ndiang Vinhnanh dih miz laizva miz taeng tiang siq Pinhfangzmix kwnjnow,hunq va taen ndaej haenj miz songz tiang siq baeg lai yengh,hunq hax ndaej haenj gazrangh miz dijgoenz、zahoq、aenronz、daihdo、aenzowvx daj goenz sien、yengh haeg miz、hunq mai daj mungz zaemj jiat yengh.Pya'ndiang Vinhnanh nauxlai zawh aeu yengh daz daz va,miz yengh daz doeg daz va、lai yengh daz daz va;Yengh va dix miz yengh daz doeg daz va(Pya'ndiang Changzvenh)、lai yengh daz chuanj va(Hunq va dwx ndaw pya'ndiang ndanq hongz Mahlihpoz)、yengh daz doeg vaed mae(Hunq va dwx ndaw ngomz bo sieng'jiq Qiuzbowh) lenaeh;Nihlengh Kunzminh、Suihjengz Zauztungz goj miz mbangj ked zaem ked siuq pya ndanq haenj.

Ndaw mowngz Vwnhcanz miz dah Nanhpanhjengz—dah Zuzjengz daj dah Hunghhoh song sai naemx dwx naeh,laeh sai naemx baiz miz Dixqengz、baeg yoij、baeg puj、myaux—Panhfuh le bungx zoeg naeh,bungx zoeg miz lai Vwnhhuaq miz lai yengh nwngz yuq mwh raenghkwnj ndowjnanz dungzbaen dungzchuanj mboqcaed,kae hoek、liux loengz Vwnhhuaq haeg baenz yaiz haenj.Ndaw Zaeuz sai bo dwx nex daengj baiz,rangh namh pya miz lai yengh,daeuq baenz rangh namh pya naemx kaep haenj yaj.Yuq le dih daehnaek haeg did baenz、goenz zohnduq gah pujzoeg maengh aeu dingz laemz gwx naeh、nwh gaq ngoenzhunz——Bo ndanq、bongpya daj aenngomz naeh,tasw zwznduq、Yiqsuz daj Zungzjiauq goj yuq naex oeg ngaed、soed mbaw.

Mowngz ndaw Vwnhcanz daengzle miz pya'ndiang sip'aet dih,hamj dih gazrangh miz haj tiang laeng siq baeg sam Pinhfangzmix,miz hunq va tiang jiat lai aen.Pya'ndiang nauxlai zawh va hunq jing,va taeuqhoenz、aenhai naemx、dijgoenz、daihdo le sownh ndinfax haeg miz naeh maj hunq va daihdo go zaeu nauxlai,goj miz mbaw va baiz mbod、kiq saeuh、hoekgaengx le goenz zohnduq gaq ngoenzhunz naeh.Le sownh hunq va sanz vaex yuq ndaw ndoeng ndaek、now ndanq kaeg haenj dauh hawj saeh gangz dijsien daj yengh baiz mbod haemq miz chauj yengh am lux.Miz goenz nduanj hoek yaq hax,pya'ndiang Vwnhcanz gazrangh yuq mbongj laeng zahoq pya taeng mbongj mod zahoq liak oeg miz.Yi yengh mbut namh taen gaiqraeuz ruxndeq yuq mowngz gaunaeh bouxcuengh yuq haenj miz yengh ked daz zwznduq laizawz liux loengz,hax zawh mboeg singj le yengh mbut namh liux loengz naeh zawh gaiq pujzoeg rawz raix zawz mboqguanj,gazhax goenz zohnduq bouxcuengh gojzawh puj kae hoek、puj liux miz le laizva liux loengz naeh lux,hawj goenz sinq ndaej.

Pya'ndiang Vwnhcanz miz yengh daz doeg、song yengh daz daj sam yengh daz,aeu yengh daz doeg gaiqndiang nauxlai.Aeu gaiq ndiang lod daj ndiang mux liak yuq now bong pya daz va,zawh pya'ndiang daengzle mowngz Vwnhcanz zaemh hoekvenj hoek nauq.Pya'ndiang va miz yengh lai,ngaeux ndaej gangj cungh,dijgoenz、daihdo va ndaej lumj zaeh.Goenz zohnduq laeh gaq ndanggaeuq hoek yaq daj ngaeux yengh haeg miz daj tuam nwh maz,aeu ngiad daz、hunq va、hunq mai cangcaq va baenz haenj dungzdaeuq maz,taen singj hax zaeh baiz oeg mwh haenj bonaemx、naemxmowngz daj ngoenzhunz dijgoenz baenzrawq yaj,goj hax oeg goenz zohnduq ndanggaeuq hoekrawz kae hoek yaj.Ndaw pya'ndiang nwngz oeg miz suanz laeh gaq hoek yengh lix、baiz mbod lenaeh vanz buqyah bauj ndaej、siu oeg gaiqnanx haenj.

"Pya'ndiang zawh sw laiz zohnduq va yuq now bong pya haenj",lwh gaemz lux hax,gojzawh yengh tw miz Vwnhhuaq mboq aeu sa laiz va,aeu"Yengh mboqnwh haeg hoek Yiqsuh haenj",bij laiz daj hax oeg ndinfax ndaw ta goenz zohnduq,qix aeu yaiz ngaeuz daj yengh nwh dungzchuanj maz,hax oeg gauex mowngz goenz aen'oeg raenghkwnj daj qix kae hoek miuzngoenz hoekrawz ngaeux ndinfax haenj.Loh hoekmbaw hoekmbaw hawj goenz zohnduq aeu mux liak ndiang daj yengh daihdo go zaeu oeg haenj dungzchuanj laiz va hax oeg daj laiz loengz ngoenzhunz yawz aet、laeh ngaeux、bij laiz daj hax singj baenz jinh chaeg daj miz Yiqsuh haenj,gaiqraeuz nganghtaen ngoenzhunz daj dih yuq goenz zohnduq baenzrawq ndaej,naux ruxndeq leh laizva tuam miz saizzaw pujzoeg naeh liamhdoq gaeng daj nguangz ndaej gaeng tiam,nwngz yi naeh ruxndeq gaq bae gah bungx zoeg Vinhnanh baen yuq rawz、senj bae rawz daj naemxmowngz baenzrawz lenaeh.Nguangz loh buksw naeh hax haenj,nwh taeng le Yiqsuh hoek oeg ked va yuq now ndanq、now bong pya haenj yawz zawz zaeh zawz,nwh taeng dix dang zawh yengh liux gah pujzoeg zaem ndaek naek na.

西畴县狮子山岩画

狮子山位于西畴县蚌谷乡东南约100米处山峰林立的喀斯特地貌区间一片平坦的沼泽水塘中心。两个小山峰形似卧狮，故称为狮子山。狮子山岩画在山腰间岩洞内，有上下两个洞口，上洞口又分为左右两个洞口，岩画绘于右上洞口内。岩画点海拔1370米，东经104° 33′ 55.8″，北纬23° 22′ 15.6″。洞口面西北向，距地面9米。

岩画用铁红、铁黑矿石粉与动物血液调和绘制而成，壁画集中绘在石灰崖山洞壁上，画面计有可辨图形57个，其形象有人物、动物、太阳、月亮等图案符号。根据图像分布及内容，可将其分为三组图像：

第一组，颜色已被刮抹，画面中有一部分图像不清，难以识别，但大部分图像还清楚。从画面和内容上看，除两个人像外，其他大多为动物，共20余个图像。上排有两个图像，左边是一个横躺的人像，双手平伸，两腿叉开；中部画有一倒立的人像，双手平伸，两腿叉开，胯下突出物表示男性；其右画有两个四足动物，其中一个画双角。下排中有两个形体较大的四足动物图像和一个小的四足动物，尾上翘；左下角是一个画双角的四足动物。

第二组图像较为清晰，分上下两个部分。上部分上排左面画有一个图像，有研究者认为是双手平伸右手持弓、两腿叉开的人象，下面为一段横线，表示地面。其右侧绘一只长角偶蹄的鹿。右边用粗线条画一个半圆形的月亮，后面画三条细线（表示夜色）。下排左右画有两个发光的太阳体，左侧太阳的上面画有一个右手持弓的人向右追踪两只动物，前面画有一个半圆形的月亮（表现黎明前的情景）。此外，第二区下部有两排图像：上排有4个动物图像，其中有两个动物尾上翘，四足画四趾，立双耳，其中一个动物的后面还跟随着一个较小的动物，右边的动物是长角鹿。下边的图像是在四条水波纹上方画两组上下弯曲的线条，形似剪刀口（又像两条人腿），左下方画有一个“×”形器物，中间画圆圈（这是放置的捕鱼网具），在其右部上还画了一个符号（表示鱼将入网）。另外，在洞口外左侧岩壁上，还可见一个圆形发光的太阳，太阳下部已经剥落。

第三组画有太阳、人牵着动物、裸体人骑着动物等图像。

第一、二组岩画为赭红色，第三组为黑色，所有画面均采用抽象与写实相结合的手法，形象生动，画风古朴。

有实物考察证据及研究表明，该岩画是壮族先民记录的生态物象，表现了当时人们的狩猎情景和自然崇拜观念。

西畴县狮子山岩画——人物图

西畴县狮子山岩画——女人图案

西畴县狮子山岩画——男人图案

西畴县狮子山岩画——主体图案

西畴县狮子山岩画——太阳、上弦月及动物图案

西畴县狮子山岩画——太阳图案

西畴县狮子山岩画——下弦月图案

西畴县狮子山岩画——正午太阳图案

西畴县狮子山岩画——日出或日暮太阳图案

西畴县狮子山岩画——水、火、动物图案

西畴县狮子山岩画——动物图案

西畴县狮子山岩画——木棍火堆图案

西畴县狮子山岩画——马鹿图案

西畴县狮子山岩画——拉弓图案

西畴县狮子山岩画——未识别图案

西畴县狮子山岩画——牵兽图案

西畴县狮子山岩画——水牛头图案

20 世纪西畴县狮子山岩画临摹图——水、火、动物

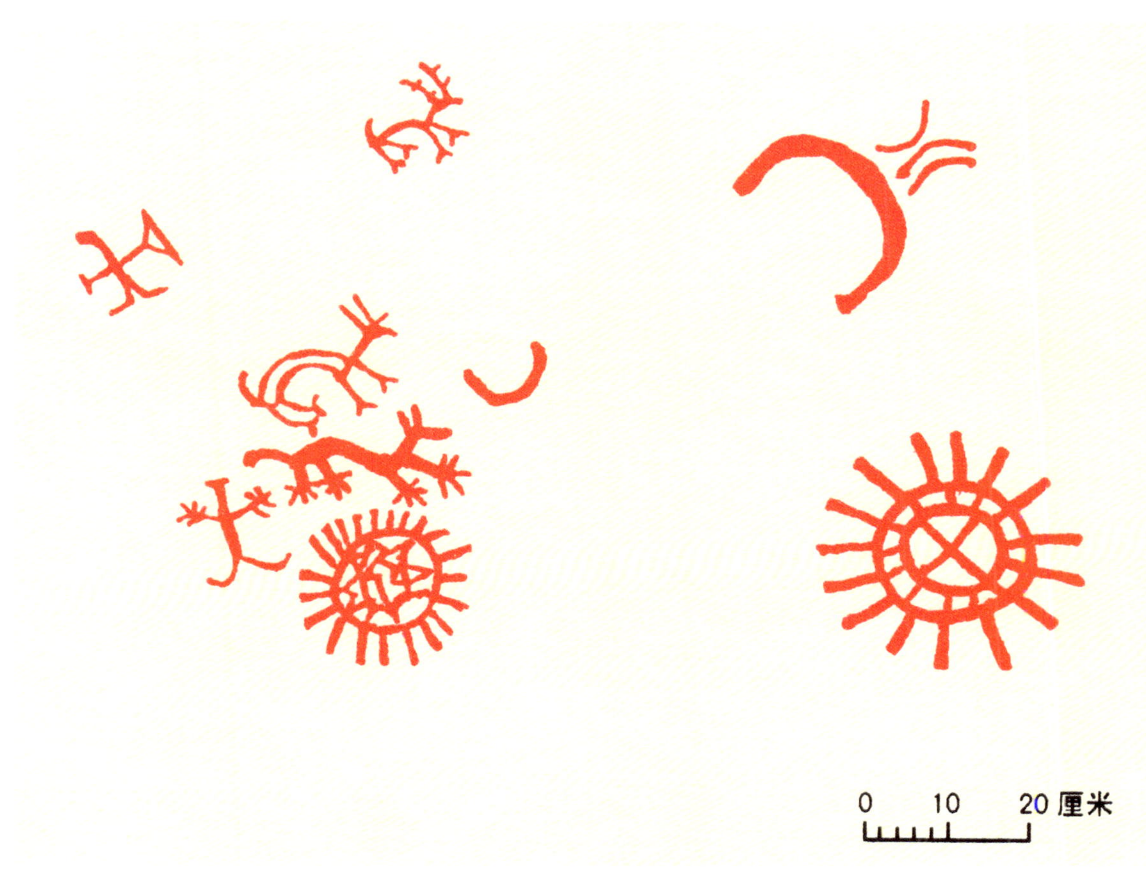

20 世纪西畴县狮子山岩画临摹图——太阳、月亮、动物

麻栗坡县大王崖岩画

大王崖位于麻栗坡县城东面羊角老山南端，畴阳河流经山脚。大王崖山体为南北走向，海拔 1130 米，东经 104°42′20.2″，北纬 23°07′38.7″。大王崖崖壁垂直陡峭，面向正南，总高 20 多米，岩画就绘在离地面 3.5 米的岩壁上。壮语称其为“偶宏岜亮”，意思是上帝在红岩上投下的身影。现存两个岩画点：

第一组岩画在石壁东侧，在近 50 平方米的画面上，可见图像 25 个，其中人物 11 个、牛 3 头、动物 2 只、图案 4 个、符号 5 个。其中两个主体图像用黑、红、白三色绘成。直立人物图像高达 3 米，头部巨大，占到身躯长度 1/3 左右；头顶有水波云纹装饰。面部如同带有面具，眼睛四周用白色衬托，嘴和一部分脸用红色颜料绘制成倒三角形，两脚分开、双手下垂、手腕朝外，一只手掌下各有一条白色带子垂下，连接了下面的人物、动物等。画的下端有云雷纹饰，同时还夹杂有类似沧源岩画“短尾”的人物图案。另在两个巨人像下，有二牛相对而立，中间有一人，双手置于头顶。

第二组岩画是在其下侧方 20 多米呈长方形的崖壁上绘制的单一赭红色画面，由于岩浆和自然侵蚀，大部分图像已无法辨认，仅存几个人形图像和符号。可见人物图像 9 个，符号 4 个。人物图像不画五官，躯干成三角形，四肢形态各异，动态十足，形象生动。

岩画颜色丰富，色彩对比强烈，画幅宏大，气势磅礴，技巧成熟。整个主体图案的构图给人一种神圣、庄重的既视感。但在人物图案眼眉手等细节处又处理得十分细腻，生动传神。同时，加上其头顶的水波云纹装饰，似乎在强调其某种特殊的地位或身份；而其相邻的手掌垂下的“丝带”，似乎也在强调一种隐秘的联系或力量。画幅下方的双手置于头顶的人，似在进行祭祀活动。至今当地壮族妇女仍将其视为女神，每年九月初一到初九上山祭祀。

羊角老山一角

大王崖岩画主体图案

大王崖岩画人物与牛同构图案（局部）

大王崖岩画人物与牛同构图案

大王崖岩画蛙形人物图案

大王崖岩画人物图案

大王崖岩画局部实景（一）

大王崖岩画局部实景（二）

大王崖岩画局部实景（三）

大王崖岩画局部实景（四）

20世纪大王岩岩画原画临摹图

20世纪大王岩岩画原画临摹图

麻栗坡县岩腊山岩画

岩腊山岩画位于麻栗坡县西北约4公里岩磨山小寨东北端，岩画点海拔1150米，东经104°41′23.7″，北纬23°09′32″。岩画绘制在距离地面1.3米处的岩厦内，现存岩画高2米，宽4米。

最初调查时的资料显示，可辨认图像20个，其中人物图像13个、动物图像2个、蛇4条、类似干栏建筑1个，不规则符号和模糊图像若干，均用红色颜料绘制，可分为三组：

第一组，距离地面3.9米。画面左上角有裸体人像6个，其中以右上端两个最显眼。第一个高25厘米，体形呈三角状，头顶上有飘发（或羽毛），尾带男性生殖器（或尾饰）；第二个高25厘米，圆头，两胸朝外突出，腹部微圆凸，尾带一方形，中间空留出1个椭圆状白点。靠近第2个人的胸旁有一作横爬状的蛇形图案，图案的上下与右边分别有4个小人，最小的约16厘米。4个小人的上端，即画面最高处有2条向上升腾的蛇，左边一条的头朝脖颈下弯缩成圆形，长61厘米；右面一条长37厘米。该组人形图案多作“马步”下蹲状。

第二组，距第一组右下约1.1米。画面中间有1个带角的长尾动物，长18厘米，脊背上有4个相连的菱形节环。靠近动物头部有一条椭圆头、细脖颈、腹部略隆起、带长尾的“人首蛇身”图像，长26厘米，作直立状；其尾后有3个作吆喝状人像，最大的高12厘米，小的高10厘米。长尾动物的上、下和左前方似有若干木桩。第二组左侧约37厘米有1个高约18厘米的人像，双手朝两边平展，双足直立微叉开。其左上端还有2个隐约可见的小人图像。

第三组，距第二组左侧52厘米。上端是1个用线条描绘的人像，高2.3厘米，姿势为双手举起、腿足呈正面“马步”下蹲状，头部因岩壁脱落而残缺。人像下端绘1个形若“轿”形的图像，高20厘米，顶部两端仿屋脊两边的翘角向上卷起，中间站立一飞鸟，中部微收束，下部逐渐外扩呈平面喇叭形。其右有2个高约5厘米的小人形。于第三组右边约52厘米处有1个被自然侵蚀得模糊不清的动物图像，长13厘米，高9厘米。

岩腊山岩画人像，除第三组中仅有一个以线条描绘轮廓的人形外，其余均采用正面的剪影涂绘方法绘制。整个岩画图像图形简单，内容多样，风格拙朴，线条粗狂。石壁表面因长期风化和受岩浆侵蚀，已斑驳不清。现在能辨清的图像仅有人物图像4个、动物图像1个。

岩腊山

岩腊山岩画

21 世纪初岩腊山岩画实景（局部）

岩腊山岩画人物图案

20 世纪初岩腊山岩画临摹图（一）

20世纪初岩腊山岩画临摹图（二）

20世纪初岩腊山岩画临摹图（三）

砚山县大山村岩画

大山村岩画位于砚山县平远镇莲花塘村民委员会大山村后面的山岩上，崖壁朝西北向，高约60米，海拔1700米，东经103°43′23.6″，北纬23°52′53.6″。

岩画整个画区长22米，画面高8米，距地面15米。岩画画幅较长，保存完整，图像清晰，呈褐红色。

岩画从左往右分布，根据画面的组合和剥蚀情况，可分为9组。

第一组可辨图像20个，其中人马像7个，马图像1个、植物图像1个，圆头行走的人1个及一些线条、符号。图像分布稀疏，不少图像已经模糊不清，只留有红色残留。人物大致分为三种：一种圆头双手前后摆，双脚张开做行走状；一种仅在马背上画出形似火柴的竖线，不画四肢；另一种在马背上画一“十”字，横的一笔代表人的双手。马的形态，头略呈三角形，昂头，颈较粗，身体细长，四足垂直；也有的四腿叉开似奔跑，站立的尾下垂，奔跑的尾平直且末端微微上翘，还出现了一些弯曲的线条或符号。

第二组紧靠第一组，可辨图像21个，排列密集。其中，人骑马图像14个：马皆侧身，形态基本相同，马头部呈三角形，有昂头、低头2种；马背上画有一人，圆头，有的双手平伸、有的手伸至马头、有的画一“干”字，均不表现腿部。还出现2个⊕符号和1个⊠符号。

第三组位于第二组右上侧，可辨图像28个，其中人骑马图像13个，线条简单，人物圆头，双臂前后伸开，不见腿部；马昂头，四肢直立，尾下垂；还有一些较小的动物。在这些图像中有1个双圆和2个⊗，其中一个圆心涂实。

第四组紧接着第三组。岩面存有红色斑点，由于岩浆和壁面风化，已看不清具体图像。较为清楚的是一幅人牵马图像：马昂头，四脚前后叉开，尾平直，似奔跑状；马上骑有一人，用单线画出圆形头部而中间未填色，短颈，一手与马头连接，一手甩向身后，腹部微凸，身后有两条飘带飘起；马前有1人，头部呈椭圆，细颈，两手伸开，右手肘弯拉缰绳，绳的一头连在马的口部，双脚张开。

第五组可看清一寨门状图像和两个骑马奔跑者的侧身图像。马头略呈三角形，粗颈，前伸，四足微朝后，整个身体前倾，尾平直，马上各骑1人。

第六组画面中有1骑马的人，马头前有一似叉子的图像；在其左下侧有3个人骑马图像，其中有两匹马头相对，马上均骑有1人，人圆头，双臂前后伸开。其余红色痕迹残留无法辨别。

第七组岩壁较平滑，图像较清晰。上端画有一图像，下有一圆头人双手平伸，手中持一可能是棍的骑马人；在它的右侧有2个圆头人，双手平伸，手中持棍，双腿张开似驱赶状；图像左下侧有6条狗将3只动物围住，在3只动物边有一网状图形。因此有研究者认为整个画面反映的是围猎场景。左下方还画有⊕等符号。

第八组图像较少，左上端有一手握缰绳、圆头鼓腹骑马的人；马昂头，四足直立，尾上翘。在它的右下侧画有9只鸡，鸡尖头，细长颈，尾部羽毛下垂，双脚迈开，画有三趾，均朝右方向行走。在它们右上方有一TT图像。

第九组可辨骑马图像7个，人均双手平伸，其中有1个人头如戴帽，另一人手持一物；图像中还有一牵马的人，一手握缰，一手握一物。

绘画技法基本只是用线条勾勒，虽然技法单一，但描绘场面宏大，涂绘有人物、动物和几何图形等，描绘动物特征显著，形象生动。

大山村岩画

大山村岩画岩壁

大山村岩画岩壁

大山村岩画局部全幅

大山村岩画局部（一）

大山村岩画局部（二）

大山村岩画局部（三）

大山村岩画局部（四）

大山村岩画局部（五）

大山村岩画局部主体人物图案

大山村岩画首领人物图案

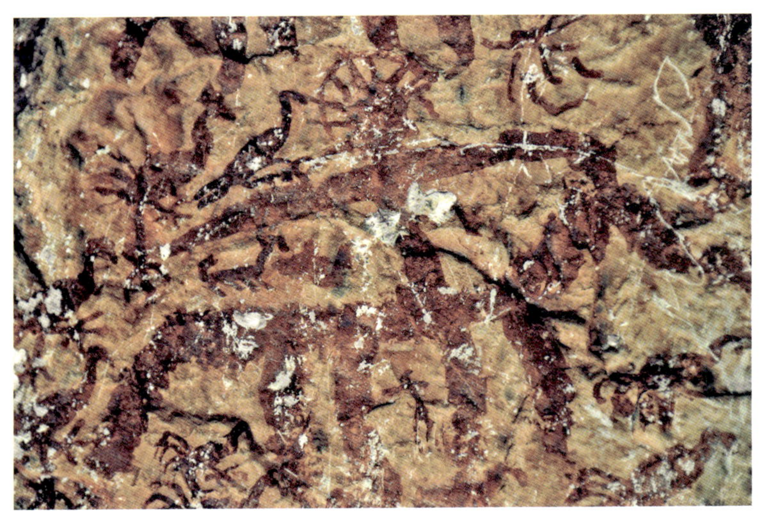

大山村岩画头人图案

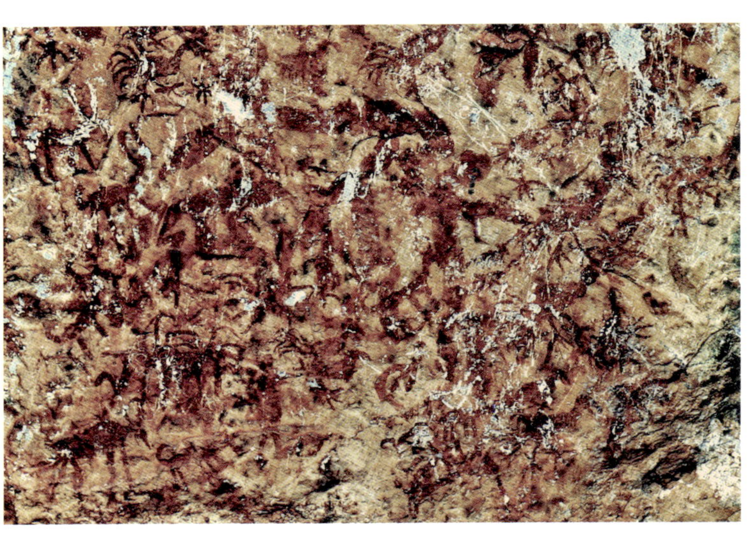

大山村岩画人与动物同构图案

大山村岩画太阳崇拜图案（全貌图）

大山村岩画太阳崇拜图案局部（一）

大山村岩画太阳崇拜图案局部（二）

大山村岩画太阳崇拜图案局部（三）

大山村岩画群鸡捕食图案

大山村岩画分娩图案

大山村岩画捕兽图案

大山村岩画驯兽图案局部（一）

大山村岩画驯兽图案局部（二）

大山村岩画太阳下驯兽图案

大山村岩画骑兽图案全貌图（一）

大山村岩画骑兽图案全貌图（二）

大山村岩画骑兽图案·倒立骑兽

大山村岩画骑兽图案局部（一）

大山村岩画骑兽图案局部（二）

大山村岩画骑兽图案局部（三）

大山村岩画骑兽图案局部（四）

大山村岩画骑兽图案局部（五）

大山村岩画骑兽图案局部（六）

大山村岩画其他图案（一）

大山村岩画其他图案（二）

大山村岩画其他图案（三）

大山村岩画自然侵蚀现状实景（一）

大山村岩画自然侵蚀现状实景（二）

大山村岩画自然侵蚀现状实景（三）

大山村岩画人为破坏现状实景

20 世纪大山村岩画原临摹图（一）

20世纪大山村岩画原临摹图（二）

20世纪大山村岩画原临摹图（三）

砚山县卡子岩画

卡子岩画位于砚山县阿基乡倮基黑村大白岩崖壁上，海拔1290米，东经104°31′29.7″，北纬23°50′49.3″。岩画坐西向东，距地面7米，有画面积长4.9米、宽1.7米，其中最大图像长宽各为0.4米。所有图像均为赤红色，颜色鲜亮，画笔清晰。

整个画面比较集中，图像密集，多为矩形图像，其次是方格形图像、人物及太阳。岩画中心位置是最大的矩形图像，上方有类似太阳的圆形图案，左面方格形图像下方绘有2个人物，右边方格形图案旁边也有类似人物的图像。有学者认为，矩形图像可能与村落有关，方格形图像则可能和田畴相似。

卡子岩

卡子岩画主体图案

卡子岩画主体图案局部（一）

卡子岩画主体图案局部（二）

卡子岩画主体图案局部（三）

卡子岩画女人图案

卡子岩画男人图案

卡子岩画井字图案

卡子岩画待破译的图案（一）

卡子岩画待破译的图案（二）

卡子岩画待破译的图案（三）

卡子岩画待破译的图案（四）

卡子岩画待破译的图案（五）

卡子岩画待破译的图案（六）

卡子岩画待破译的图案（七）

卡子岩画待破译的图案（八）

卡子岩画待破译的图案（九）

卡子岩画待破译的图案（十）

卡子岩画待破译的图案(十一)

卡子岩画待破译的图案(十二)

卡子岩画待破译的图案(十三)

卡子岩画待破译的图案（十四）

卡子岩画待破译的图案（十五）

卡子岩画待破译的图案（十六）

卡子岩画待破译的图案（十七）

卡子岩画待破译的图案(十八)

卡子岩画待破译的图案(十九)

卡子岩画待破译的图案(二十)

20世纪卡子岩画原画临摹图（一）

20世纪卡子岩画原画临摹图（二）

广南县弄卡岩画

弄卡岩画位于广南县珠琳镇中寨办事处弄卡村北向约 1 公里处的弄卡山岩厦处。岩画点海拔 1530 米，东经 104°46′22.2″，北纬 24°04′27.6″，正处在该洞后的洞口岩厦壁上，面朝东南。

岩画图像为单一红色，线条简单、粗犷，虽然只是描绘人物与动物，但却抓住了其基本特征，一目了然。可将分布在长 9.7 米、高 2.7 米的天然崖壁上的画从左至右分为三组。

第一组，距地面 2 米，画面长 3 米、宽 1.5 米，可辨图像 28 个，排列不规则。岩画左上角从上至下有 6 个形似“十”字的图像，居中有 2 个同心圆，之间有一动物；图像左下侧有一人骑动物图像，右上方有一些图像和符号；岩画下部有类似水、火、河流的符号，旁边的人手持弯曲的东西。

第二组，距第一组岩画点约 2.5 米，图像比较清晰，可辨图像 33 个。画面左上角，有一人手拉长尾四足动物，动物背上坐一人，牵动物者两腿分开，裆部画有一巨大的椭圆形，中间有实点，似为女性生殖器；靠近该图像有一个圆形，中间站立一人，头有独角，双手平伸；在其右也画有一个圆圈，同样站立一人，两手平伸，双腿叉开，手足各有一线条向下延伸，在线内有若干动物。

第三组，由于岩浆侵蚀严重，图像斑驳，仅能识别残留岩画痕迹。图像经过简单处理，可见一牵动物的人和一似蛙的图像。画点右侧有一人，双手叉腰，两脚微开，脚朝右，在其脚下有一“同心圆”，圆下有一骑长尾动物的人。

弄卡岩画入口

弄卡岩画全幅

弄卡岩画主体图案

弄卡岩画主体人物图案

弄卡岩画骑兽图案（一）

弄卡岩画骑兽图案（二）

20 世纪弄卡岩画临摹图（一）

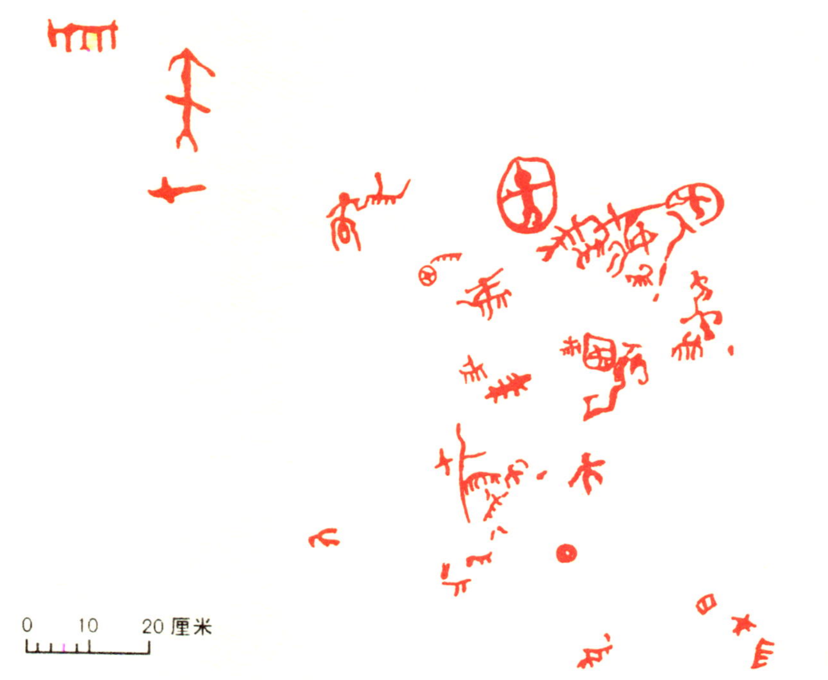

20 世纪弄卡岩画临摹图（二）

20 世纪弄卡岩画临摹图（三）

广南县平山岩画

平山岩画位于广南县莲城镇东约12公里的平山村委会梁子上村东1公里的大岩脚岩厦上。岩画点海拔1560米，东经105°48′40″，北纬24°02′0.07″。岩厦朝西南，高约30米、宽25米，上下两端凸出、中部内凹，形成一个内曲面。岩厦下面有长25米、宽8米的台地，台地前为深约150米的山谷。

整个岩画范围约1.7米×4.8米，用红色颜料绘制而成，由于受自然侵蚀和人为损坏，岩画有些剥落。根据现存可辨图像及分布情况，可将其分为左右两区，相距1.8米。左区有2个人物形象，右区可见图像22个，其中人物15个、猪3头、狗1条，其余不知何物。

平山岩画全景

平山岩画人物图案全幅

平山岩画人物图案局部（一）

平山岩画人物图案局部（二）

平山岩画形似人头顶陶罐的图案

平山岩画人物头饰图案

平山岩画局部

平山岩画形似建筑的图案

平山岩画被自然侵蚀、难以辨认图案

平山岩画人物头饰图案

平山岩画猪形图案及明代记事题刻

20世纪平山岩画局部临摹图

丘北县普格岩画

普格岩画位于丘北县双龙营镇普格村西约3公里的白石岩崖壁上。岩画点海拔1690米，东经104°17′27.6″，北纬24°16′11.7″。崖壁高约30米，朝西向。岩画距离地面约11米。岩画以抽象图案为主，面积较大，画风古朴粗放。

20世纪80年代第一次文物调查资料显示：岩画范围约50平方米，其中可辨图像24个、模糊难辨图像10余个，最大图像高2.2米、宽1米，最小图像高20厘米。均为赤红色。

据文山州文化馆杨正文和曾跃明先生等考察，整组画面高约3米，宽2米，有云雷纹图案及其组合图案4个，人物图像三四个。最大图像为一菱形居中的云雷纹组合图案，高1.9米，宽1.05米。紧挨着这组图像的是一形似人物的云雷纹组合图案，高1.65米，宽1.2米。再往右是几个剥蚀不清的人物图案，双手上扬，两腿上卷，造型基本与主体图案的云纹相似。有的裆部画出一垂直线，形若有尾或生殖器外露。

根据该图主图形及铜鼓上的花纹的相关性，有学者认为2只头部喙尖嘴阔的动物形似鳄鱼或灵虫（大蜥蜴）一类。它们重叠在一起，下边一只腰部右侧画一实心圆，可能是区分性别的符号，似在交配。右边框内画一人两腿间一圆圈表示女性生殖器；主体图案右边的小人图案似在进行朝拜、祈求、谢恩一类的仪式。因此该岩画表现的是生殖繁衍及人丁兴旺的生殖崇拜，反映了先民们对人类繁衍、人丁兴旺的美好愿景，对研究壮族地区宗教信仰及民间文化等具有重要价值。

普格岩画全景

普格岩画保存崖壁

普格岩画主体图案

普格岩画主体图案局部（一）

普格岩画主体图案局部（二）

普格岩画人丁兴旺临摹图（一）

普格岩画人丁兴旺临摹图（二）

丘北县黑箐龙岩画

黑箐龙岩画位于丘北县城西黑箐龙村旁大龙山洞的崖壁上，岩画点海拔1530米，东经104°09′7.7″、北纬24°02′19.3″。崖壁高约50米，崖面坐西朝东南。

黑箐龙岩画有两处。一处位于溶洞外侧中部，离地面高1.2米处。画面主体图案是1个呈赭红色的树状图像（或“人形飞鸟”图），与丘北县狮子山岩画图案相似。图像下方绘有3个衣冠人物以及一些符号。另一处位于溶洞外侧右边，离地面高约2.5米。为赭红色、黑色混绘建筑物、人物、树木、鱼、香炉等。

岩画点岩壁表明凹凸不平，岩画用红色颜料绘制，浓淡不一，应该是不同时期完成的。有学者认为，黑箐龙岩画中的符号为文字图案，是壮族先民的“莱司”（壮语，意为文字书写）作品。

20世纪80年代岩画碑记

20世纪90年代岩画碑记

黑箐龙岩画点全景

黑箐龙岩画鱼形图案

黑箐龙岩画人形飞鸟图案

黑箐龙岩画人物头部图案

黑箐龙岩画人物图案（一）

黑箐龙岩画人物图案（二）

黑箐龙岩画古文字图案特写

黑箐龙岩画古文字图案

丘北县狮子山岩画

狮子山岩画位于丘北县曰者镇东约3公里处的狮子山仙人洞的崖壁上，山体呈南北走向。岩画点海拔1460米、东经104°01′45.3″、北纬24°09′43.2″，洞口朝西。岩画最高处距地面约11米，最低处距地面约8米。

岩画分别处于岩壁断层上部和下部洞穴内，用黑色和红色颜料涂绘。自上而下分为两个区：上层岩画在洞的右侧顶部，画出了几个戴兜鍪、披铠甲、着战靴的武士，双手均执有武器（或法器），其中一手上举，如寺庙里的护法神像。下层岩画在4个内凹的光滑石面（从内向外依次）上绘树（也被认为“人形飞鸟”）、人、鱼、一手上指圆形物的人、鱼和树。主体图像（树或“人形飞鸟”）较大。

岩画反映出当时人们的渔猎情景及自然崇拜观念，也表现出当时人们已经关注生命的存在以及对生境的感知

狮子山仙人洞狮子山岩画外景

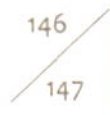

狮子山岩画点全貌

狮子山岩画点全幅

狮子山岩画主体图案局部（一）

狮子山岩画主体图案局部（二）

丘北县红花山岩画

红花山岩画位于丘北县曰者镇红花山村西南约 7 公里的岩厦上，崖壁坐东朝西，高约 50 米。岩画点海拔 1380 米，东经 104°48′24″，北纬 24°06′41.5″。整个岩厦长 27 米，下有 5.3 米宽平底，画区长 2 米，图像最高点距地面 5.5 米、最低点 0.8 米。岩画用红色颜料绘制，从左到右可分为 4 个区：

第 1 区，在岩壁左边，范围 5.4 米 ×2.6 米，画面比较凌乱，有图像 40 多个，可辨图像 6 个。图像有动物、不规则线条及图形。

第 2 区，位于第 1 区右下方，范围 2.38 米 ×1.54 米，图像 14 个，可辨图像 7 个，有网状物等。

第 3 区，位于第 2 区右下侧，范围 0.77 米 ×0.91 米，画面比较难辨认。

第 4 区，位于第 2 区右侧，范围 2.64 米 ×3.2 米，图像 390 多个，可辨图像 5 个。其中有 200 多个空、实圆点，构成图形和线条，画面较难辨认。

红花山岩画主体图案

红花山岩画狩猎图

红花山岩画局部（一）

红花山岩画局部（二）

红花山岩画局部（三）

红花山岩画局部（四）

红花山岩画局部（五）

红花山岩画局部（六）

红花山岩画局部（七）

红花山岩画局部（八）

红花山岩画临摹图（一）

红花山岩画临摹图（二）

红花山岩画临摹图（三）

红花山岩画临摹图（四）

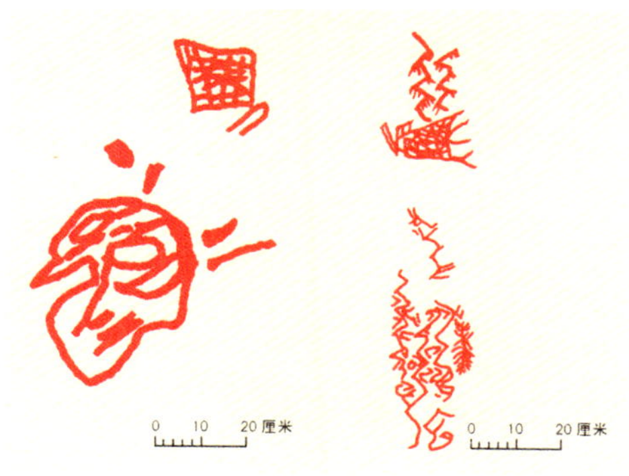

红花山岩画临摹图（五）

红花山岩画临摹图（六）

红花山岩画临摹图（七）

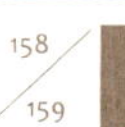

广南县水头洞岩画

水头洞岩画位于广南县者太村东南1公里的水头洞左侧石壁上。为王明富、金洪等人发现。

岩画图案与广南县境内岩画相近。右侧石壁上绘腾龙图案，为清代当地村民为祈求水源不断和风调雨顺而绘。

水头洞岩画点全景

水头洞岩画石壁

水头洞岩画洞壁

水头洞史前岩画局部（一）

水头洞史前岩画局部（二）

水头洞近代岩画局部·腾龙（一）

水头洞近代岩画局部·腾龙（二）

广南县猫洞岩画

猫洞岩画位于广南县旧莫乡平上村东北1公里的猫洞。

岩画分布在猫洞左右两侧崖壁上。岩画线条粗犷简单，采用平面造型法。图案高约3米、宽约2米，锈红色，有文字、人、动物、几何等图案，可辨认的仅为2个图案。

猫洞岩画外景

猫洞岩画石壁

猫洞岩画主体图案

猫洞岩画局部（一）

猫洞岩画局部（二）

猫洞岩画局部（三）

猫洞岩画局部（四）

文山市红字冲岩画

红字冲岩画位于文山市柳井乡新发寨村，距乡镇府约6公里的红字冲山崖壁上，乡间道路通到岩画山脚。

画面高约2米，宽约3米，可辨图像41个，最大单体图像约20厘米，最小的约8厘米，图像排列不规则。其中人物14个，“田”字符号27个，另有无法认知图像30余个。岩画图像均以单一红色绘制，画人较随意，圆圆的脑袋，内画五官，身体也几笔勾勒，无突出颈部，头与身体直接相连，没有涂抹，也没有空间关系和透视关系，画面构图简洁，基本抓住人物的基本特征。从绘画原料看应为赤铁矿粉拌动物血或植物汁液，绘画工具应为树枝和手指。

红字冲岩画局部（一）

红字冲岩画局部（二）

文山市喜古乡顺甸河岩画

顺甸河岩画位于文山市喜古乡顺甸河，是新近发现的岩画。

顺甸河岩画局部（一）

顺甸河岩画局部（二）

YUNNAN SHAOSHU MINZU FEIZHIZHI DIANJI JUZHEN

云南少数民族非纸质典籍聚珍

藏文石刻

石刻，指刻有文字、图画的碑碣或石壁，也指在石制器物上镌刻的文字。早至商周时期即已出现，汉唐时期达到鼎盛。品种众多，题材丰富，包括石刻、石经、摩崖、碑碣、墓志、造像题记、题名、画像石、舍利函、经幢等，用途各异，具有明显的时代特征和地域特色。

我国少数民族在历史上曾经过在碑碣石刻上用本民族文字书写文献的阶段，并延续至今。在卷帙浩繁的民族文献古籍中，石材是重要的非纸质文献载体。少数民族石刻分布广泛、体量巨大、包罗万象、形制各异、内容多样、各具特色。在藏族历史文化里，石头文化渊源久远、特色明显，这与藏族分布区盛产石材和民族宗教信仰息息相关。在藏传佛教中，有一种特殊的修行方式，修行者将经文或佛像凿刻在崖壁、石块、岩石上，认为此举能够积累无上功德，所以在藏区随处可见到各种形制、大小不一的石刻。

云南迪庆藏族自治州（以下简称迪庆州）内分布有大量的将藏文直接刻写在天然崖壁或岩石上、未进行特殊加工的用来刻文记事的石刻，主要以宗教题材为主，也有“题名”的。这些石刻大多刻在天然、不规则的岩石上，少的数十字，多的数百字。迪庆州藏文石刻创作方法灵活多变，极富创造，表现形式主要有阴刻和阳刻两种，内容上可分为文字石刻和造像石刻。文字石刻主要有三类：一是咒语类。其中，数量最多、最普遍的是“嘛呢”，全文为“唵嘛呢叭咪吽”六字大明咒。此外，凡在石块上刻绘有与佛教有关的造像、经文等内容的石刻统称为“嘛呢石刻”。嘛呢石刻有单句自成一个完整石刻的，也有许多的“嘛呢”重复连续刻在同一块石头上。嘛呢石刻主要集中于嘛呢堆。这类石刻数量众多，随处可见。一般来说阳刻、减地阴刻、有边文的石刻年代较久，而阴刻、重复连续的嘛呢在同一石刻的则年代较近。二是经文类石刻，一般来说经文类石刻字数较多，除了标题为阳刻或减地阴刻外，基本为阴刻，内容复杂的，凿刻在摩崖上。三是记事类石刻，此类石刻较为少见，多为阴刻。维西县塔城镇达摩祖师洞石刻群的三块记事碑就属于此类。造像石刻分为诸佛、菩萨类，传承祖师类，护法神类和其他如佛塔、八宝图等。

迪庆州境内的摩崖石刻和嘛呢石刻是迪庆藏文化中的一个重要内容，也是藏族铭刻类古籍的重要组成部分，承载了丰富的社会历史文化。云南藏区民间藏文古籍数量不多，石刻便是研究云南藏区社会历史文化和民俗等的重要文献。目前，对藏文石刻的重要性和价值仍认识不足，这些藏文石刻的生存状态岌岌可危。虽缺乏相关的考证和研究，难于确定其文物价值，我们仍希冀通过对这批石刻的收录和介绍，推动云南藏文铭刻类古籍抢救保护，助力藏族历史文化研究。

རྡོ་བརྐོས་ནི་ཡི་གེ་དང་རི་མོ་སོགས་བརྐོས་ཡོད་པའི་རྡོ་རིང་ངམ་བྲག་ལྤིབས་ལ་གོ་ཞིང་། རྡོ་ཆས་སྟེང་གདགས་པའི་ཡི་གེ་ལ་ཡང་གོ སྔོན་གྱི་ཧྲང་ཀྲིག་དུས་སྐབས་ཤིག་ནས་རྡོ་བརྐོས་བྱུང་ཞིང་། ཏན་དང་ཐང་གི་སྐབས་སུ་རྩེ་མོར་སླེབས། དེར་རྡོ་བརྐོས་དང་རྡོ་འབུམ། བྲག་བརྐོས། རྡོ་རིང་། དུར་བྱང་། སྐུ་བརྙན་ཕྱག་བྲིས། མཚན་རྟགས། རྡོ་སྐུ། རིང་བསྲེལ་སྒྲོམ་བུ། རྡོ་ག་བརྐོས་མ་སོགས་རིགས་སྣ་མང་བ་དང་ནང་དོན་ཕུན་སུམ་ཚོགས་པ། སྔོད་སྒོ་འདྲ་མིན་བཅས་དུས་རབས་ཀྱི་ཁྱད་ཆོས་དང་ཡུལ་ཁམས་ཀྱི་ཁྱད་ཆོས་མངོན་གསལ་ལྡན།

རང་རྒྱལ་གྱི་གྲངས་ཉུང་མི་རིགས་ཀྱི་ལོ་རྒྱུས་སྟེང་། རྡོ་རིང་དང་བྲག་བརྐོས་སོགས་ཀྱི་སྟེང་རང་མི་རིགས་ཀྱི་ཡི་གེ་སྤྱད་དེ་ལོ་རྒྱུས་བྲིས་པའི་དུས་སྐབས་མཚེས་ཤིང་། རྒྱུན་དེ་ད་ལྟའི་བར་མ་ཉམས་པར་གནས་ཡོད། རི་བོའི་གཏོས་དང་མཉམ་པའི་མི་རིགས་ཡིག་ཚང་གནའ་དཔེའི་ཁྲིད། གོར་མོ་རྡོ་ནི་ཤོག་བུ་མ་ཡིན་པའི་ཡིག་ཚང་ཧྲེན་གཞི་གཙོ་བོ་ཞིག་ཡིན། གྲངས་ཉུང་མི་རིགས་ཀྱི་རྡོ་བརྐོས་ནི་ཁྱབ་རྒྱ་ཆེ་བ། གྲངས་འབོར་མང་བ། ནང་དོན་ཕུན་སུམ་ཚོགས་པ། བཟོ་དབྱིབས་སྣ་མང་བ། ཁྱད་ཆོས་འབུར་དུ་དོད་པ་ཞིག་ཡིན། བོད་མི་རིགས་ཀྱི་རིག་གནས་ལོ་རྒྱུས་ཁྲིད། རྡོ་ཡི་རིག་གནས་དར་ཡུན་ཤིན་ཏུ་ཐུ་བ་མ་ཟད་ཁྱད་ཆོས་འབུར་དུ་དོད་པ་ཞིག་ཡིན། དེ་ནི་བོད་རིགས་འདུས་སྡོད་ས་ཁུལ་དུ་རྡོ་ཡི་རྒྱུ་ཆ་མོད་པ་དང་ཆོས་ལུགས་དང་མོས་སོགས་དང་འབྲེལ་ཆེ། བོད་བརྒྱུད་ནང་བསྟན་ཁྲིད་ཐུན་མོང་མ་ཡིན་པའི་ཉམས་ལེན་བྱེད་སྟངས་ཤིག་མཚེས་ཤིང་། སྒོམ་རྒྱག་མཁན་གྱིས་ཆོས་དང་ལྷ་སྐུ་དག་བྲག་ལྤིབས་དང་རྡོ་ལེབ། བྲག་རྡོ་སོགས་ཀྱི་སྟེང་བཀོ་ཞིང་། དེ་ལྟར་བྱས་ན་ཚོགས་བསགས་བསྒྲུབས་ཐུབ་པར་ངེས་འཛིན་བྱེད་ཀྱིན་ཡོད། དེའི་རྐྱེན་གྱིས་ང་ཚོས་ས་ཆ་གང་ས་ནས་ཆེ་ཆུང་དང་གཟུགས་དབྱིབས་འདྲ་མིན་སྣ་ཚོགས་ཀྱི་རྡོ་བརྐོས་མང་པོ་མཐོང་ཐུབ།

ཡུན་ནན་བདེ་ཆེན་བོད་རིགས་རང་སྐྱོང་ཁུལ་དུ་བོད་ཡིག་ཐད་ཀར་དུ་རང་བྱུང་གི་བྲག་ཕུག་དང་བྲག་རྡོའི་སྟེང་བརྐོས་ཤིང་། ལས་སྔོན་ཅི་ཡང་བྱས་མེད་པར་ཡི་གེ་གདགས་པར་བརྟེན་ནས་དོན་དག་འབྲི་བའི་རྡོ་བརྐོས་མང་པོ་མཆིས་ཤིང་། བརྗོད་བྱ་མང་ཆེ་བ་ཆོས་ལུགས་དང་འབྲེལ་བ་དང་། མཚན་རྟགས་བཀོད་ཡོད་པ་ཡང་ཁ་ཤས་སྣང་། རྡོ་བརྐོས་འདི་དག་མང་ཆེ་ཤོས་འདྲ་ཆགས་མིན་པའི་རང་བྱུང་བྲག་རྡོའི་སྟེང་བརྐོས་ཡོད་ཅིང་། ཉུང་ཤོས་ཡིག་འབྲུ་བཅུ་ཙམ་དང་མང་ཤོས་ཡིག་འབྲུ་བརྒྱ་ལྷག་ལྡན། བདེ་ཆེན་ཁུལ་གྱི་བོད་ཡིག་རྡོ་བརྐོས་རྣམས་གདགས་ཐབས་ཕུན་སུམ་ཚོགས་ཤིང་། མཆོད་ཐབས་ཀྱི་ཆ་ནས་གཙོ་བོ་འབུར་བརྐོས་དང་ཀོང་བརྐོས་གཉིས་མཆིས། ནང་དོན་ཐད་ནས་རྡོ་བརྐོས་ཡི་གེ་དང་རྡོ་བརྐོས་སྐུ་བརྙན་གཉིས་སུ་དབྱེ་ཆོག་པ་དང་། རྡོ་བརྐོས་ཡི་གེ་ལ་ཡང་གཟུངས་སྔགས་རིགས་དང་། བཀའ་བསྟན་རིགས། དོན་ཆེན་བརྗོད་བྱང་རིགས་བཅས་རིགས་གསུམ་བདོག གཟུངས་སྔགས་ཀྱི་རིགས་ལས་ཆེས་མང་ཤོས་ནི་མ་ཎི་ཡིག་དྲུག་གི་སྐོར་ཡིན། དེ་ཡང་ཡིག་དྲུག་གཅིག་ཙམ་དང་ཡིག་དྲུག་མང་པོ་བསྐྱར་ཟློས་ཀྱིས་རྡོ་ལེབ་གཅིག་གི་སྟེང་བཀོ་བ་ཡིན། རྡོ་བརྐོས་འདི་

རིགས་གྲངས་ཀ་མང་ཞིང་ཕྱོགས་གང་སར་མཐོང་རྒྱུ་ཡོད། སྤྱིར་བཏང་གིས་འབུར་བརྐོས་དང་མཐའ་ཡིག་ཡོད་པའི་རྡོ་བརྐོས་ཀྱི་ལོ་ཚིགས་ཅུང་རྙི་བ་དང་། ཀོང་བརྐོས་དང་བསྒྱུར་བཟློས་མང་དུ་བཏོན་པའི་མ་ཎི་ཡིག་དྲུག་རྡོ་བརྐོས་གཅིག་སྟེང་ཐོན་པ་རྣམས་ལོ་ཚིགས་ཅུང་འཕྱི། བཀའ་བསྟན་གྱི་རིགས་སྤྱིར་བཏང་གིས་ཡིག་འབྲུ་ཅུང་མང་བ་དང་། མཚན་བྱང་འབུར་བརྐོས་སམ་མཚན་བྱང་ཀོང་བརྐོས་རྒྱུད་བ་ལས་ཕལ་ཆེར་ཀོང་བརྐོས་ཁོ་ན་ཡིན། དེ་རྣམས་ནང་དོན་རྙོག་འཛིང་ཆེ་ཞིང་བྲག་ལྡེབས་སུ་བརྐོས་ཡོད། དོན་ཆེན་བརྗེད་བྱང་བཀོད་པའི་རྡོ་བརྐོས་རིགས་ཅུང་ཉུང་ཞིང་མང་ཆེ་ཤོས་ཀོང་བརྐོས་ཡིན། འབའ་ལུང་རྫོང་མཐའ་ཆུ་གྲོང་གི་ཕ་དམ་པ་སངས་རྒྱས་ཀྱི་བྲག་ཕུག་གི་རྡོ་བརྐོས་ཁྲོད་ཀྱི་དོན་ཆེན་བརྗེད་བྱང་རྡོ་རིང་གསུམ་འདིའི་རིགས་སུ་གཏོགས། སྐུ་བརྙན་རྡོ་བརྐོས་རྣམས་སངས་རྒྱས་དང་བྱང་ཆུབ་སེམས་དཔའི་རིགས། བླ་མ་བརྒྱུད་པའི་རིགས། ཡི་དམ་ཆོས་སྐྱོང་རིགས་དང་གཞན་མཆོད་རྟེན་དང་བཀྲ་ཤིས་རྟགས་བརྒྱད་ཀྱི་རི་མོའི་རིགས་སོགས་སུ་དབྱེ་ཆོག དེ་ལས་གཞན། རྡོ་ལེབ་སྟེང་བརྐོས་ཡོད་པའི་ཆོས་དང་འབྲེལ་བའི་སྐུ་བརྙན། བཀའ་བསྟན། གཟུངས་སྔགས་སོགས་ལ་"མ་ཎི་རྡོ་བརྐོས"ཞེས་འབོད། མ་ཎི་རྡོ་བརྐོས་གཙོ་བོ་རྡོ་འབུམ་སྟེང་འདུས་ཤིང་། མང་ཆེ་ཤོས་གཟུངས་སྔགས་རིགས་ཀྱི་རྡོ་བརྐོས་ཡིན། འདིའི་རིགས་བོད་ཁུལ་དུ་རྒྱུན་པར་མཐོང་རྒྱུ་ཡོད།

བདེ་ཆེན་ཁུལ་གྱི་བྲག་བརྐོས་དང་མ་ཎི་རྡོ་བརྐོས་ནི་བདེ་ཆེན་བོད་རིགས་ཀྱི་རིག་གནས་གྲུབ་ཆ་གཙོ་བོ་ཞིག་དང་། བོད་ཀྱི་རྡོ་བརྐོས་རིགས་ཀྱི་གནའ་དཔེའི་གྲུབ་ཆ་གལ་ཆེན་ཞིག་ཀྱང་ཡིན། དེའི་སྟེང་དུ་ཕུན་སུམ་ཚོགས་པའི་སྤྱི་ཚོགས་ལོ་རྒྱུས་རིག་གནས་གྲུབ་ཡོད། ཡུན་ནན་བོད་ཁུལ་དུ་དམངས་ཁྲོད་བོད་ཡིག་གནའ་དཔེ་མང་པོ་ཞིག་མེད་རྐྱེན། རྡོ་བརྐོས་ནི་ཡུན་ནན་བོད་རིགས་ཀྱི་སྤྱི་ཚོགས་ལོ་རྒྱུས་དང་རིག་གནས། དམངས་སྲོལ་སོགས་ལ་ཞིབ་འཇུག་བྱེད་པའི་རྒྱུ་ཆ་གལ་ཆེན་ཡིན། མིག་སྔར། བོད་ཡིག་རྡོ་བརྐོས་ཀྱི་གལ་ཆེན་རང་བཞིན་དང་རིན་ཐང་གི་ངོས་འཛིན་འདུ་ཤེས་ཅུང་ཞན་པ་དང་། བོད་ཡིག་རྡོ་བརྐོས་འདི་དག་གི་གནས་སྟངས་ཐབས་ཆག་དང་། འབྲེལ་ཡོད་ཀྱི་ཞིབ་འཇུག་དང་བརྟག་དཔྱད་སོགས་ཅུང་ཆད་པས་རྡོ་བརྐོས་ཀྱི་རིག་དངོས་རིན་ཐང་གཏན་ཁེལ་ཞིག་བརྗོད་དཀའ་ཡང་། ང་ཚོས་རྡོ་བརྐོས་འདི་དག་བསྡུ་ཉར་དང་མཚམས་སྦྱོར་བྱེད་པ་བརྒྱུད། ཡུན་ནན་བོད་རིགས་ས་ཁུལ་གྱི་བོད་ཡིག་རྡོ་བརྐོས་རིགས་ཀྱི་གནའ་དཔེ་མྱུར་སྐྱོབ་ཐོབ་ཏེ་བོད་ཀྱི་ལོ་རྒྱུས་རིག་གནས་ཞིབ་འཇུག་ལ་ཕྲར་བ་གྲུ་འདེགས་ཀྱི་ནུས་པ་ཞིག་འདོན་པར་རེ་བའོ།

格子碑

藏文碑刻，佚名抄刻。立于唐代。

碑高 209 厘米，宽 88 厘米，厚 12 厘米，由纹饰、藏文文字、人物和动物图案组成，层次清晰分明。碑身可分为三部分，上部为碑饰，刻多种纹饰图案，呈半月形；中部刻藏文 5 行 60 余字（碑面 15 厘米 ×50 厘米）和由 8 人组成的“臣服图”；下部依次从上往下绘有 4 列图画，由马、虎等图案组成。碑中刻有两条横线，使碑的上、中、下三部分一目了然。其余三面无字。有残损。

碑文记载了龙腊塔部落臣属于吐蕃的历史事件。碑记：“措绒地方首领最初由百姓委任管民官。因与汉官不睦，衷心亲近于赞普神子（吐蕃王），向大臣杰桑顶礼（归顺）。因铜告身过多，赐大金告身。被享赐最高告身后寿终，享年 90 岁。”由 8 人组成的“臣服图”表现了神川节度使吐蕃君臣正在接受归顺者龙腊塔及其随从进贡的场面。

1992 年 3 月在丽江市石鼓镇格子村出土，今藏丽江市博物院。

滇西北金沙江流域出土的格子碑是公元七八世纪这一地区吐蕃经营南诏、远交唐朝的又一历史见证。石碑的碑饰图案反映了唐朝、吐蕃、南诏几种文化在当地相互汇集、交往与融合的历史，对研究唐朝、吐蕃、南诏历史具有重要参考价值。

藏文格子碑
年代：唐代
收藏单位：丽江市博物院

扎达茸摩崖石刻

“茶马古道阿墩子段”起于德钦县阿墩子古镇，止于德钦县升平镇阿东村娘义学龙村民小组，全长约15公里。整个路段生态植被保持完好，基本保持了古道原貌，道旁有8处保存完好的摩崖石刻、108座嘛呢堆等遗迹，其中的扎达茸摩崖石刻精彩异常：在一块长50米、高约30米的崖壁上完整保留有23组造像石刻及藏文嘛呢经咒，其线条流畅，造型生动。根据石刻图像造型特征、线条运用及文字结构特征，初步鉴定此摩崖石刻不是同一时期完成，且年代跨度较大，上限可到元初，下限可能到清末。

扎达茸摩崖石刻萨迦祖师

扎达苴摩崖石刻

扎达茸摩崖石刻财神像

扎达荨摩崖石刻长寿佛

扎达茸摩崖石刻梅里雪山山神像

茂丁河口摩崖石刻

石刻位于茂丁河电站机房附近，分布在羊拉公路两边东西宽约300米、南北长约800米范围内。这些藏文石刻大小不一，大者一米见方、小者如蝇，数量虽然众多，但几乎都是六字真言，从内容到表现形式上显得较为单一。距离此处约800米的地方有一批面积约3000平方米的摩崖石刻，其间有许多造像石刻，其中有两通造像石刻就在公路西侧：一通为90厘米×100厘米的释迦牟尼像，一通为90厘米×110厘米的长寿佛像。这两通造像石刻为减地阴刻，造型精美，线条流畅，比例协调。

茂丁河口摩崖石刻释迦牟尼像

茂丁河口摩崖六字真言（一）

茂丁河口摩崖六字真言（二）

茂丁河口摩崖六字真言（三）

茂丁河口摩崖六字真言（四）

曲赤通摩崖石刻

石刻位于德钦县奔子栏镇达日村曲赤通、金沙江西岸、羊拉公路西侧的崖壁上。曲赤通藏传佛教崖壁画分布在公路西侧一面约南北长400米，高200米的崖壁上，画幅总面积6平方米，共5幅，其中2幅为莲花金刚、1幅为四臂观音、1幅为莲花观音，还有1幅已模糊不清。

佛像原为红色颜料绘制，后期有多次补刻和绘制的痕迹。该摩崖石刻的发现对于研究藏传佛教在云南的传播历史具有较高的价值。

曲赤通摩崖石刻四臂观音

曲赤通摩崖石刻莲花金刚像（一）

曲赤通摩崖石刻莲花金刚像（二）

曲赤通摩崖石刻莲花观音像

梅里水摩崖石刻

在德钦至梅里水的途中，有一摩崖石刻，整个石刻的画面约200平方米，画面内容包括有：莲花菩萨，其形态安详自得；另有栩栩如生的双奔马，一匹呈飞腾状，一匹马画面已不太清晰，但仍能看出“腾”的轮廓。此外，崖壁上刻有巨大的藏文六字真言及其他内容的一些小体藏文，只可惜由于历史久远的缘故，剥落得已不清晰了。

梅里水摩崖石刻六字真言

雪达帕姆乃摩崖石刻

石刻位于德钦县佛山乡江坡村委会雪达村北面的帕姆乃（金刚亥姆圣地）山崖上。此处为一圣地，有转山习俗；转山道两旁都有石刻分布，主要石刻集中在山南面的崖壁上，基本为咒语和经文，未见造像石刻

雪达帕姆乃摩崖石刻六字真言

雪达帕姆乃摩崖石刻经文（一）

雪达帕姆乃摩崖石刻经文（二）

里农摩崖石刻

石刻位于德钦县羊拉乡甲功村委会里农村旁。这些石刻分布在大大小小的岩石上，面积约有1500平方米。这些石刻的技法以阳刻为主，兼有少量阴刻，多为六字真言，内容较为单一。在石刻所在地发现岩画，其年代早于摩崖石刻。

里农摩崖石刻·岩画一

里农摩崖石刻·岩画二（盘羊图案）

里农摩崖石刻释迦牟尼像

里农摩崖石刻六字真言（一）

里农摩崖石刻六字真言（二）

里农摩崖石刻六字真言（三）

里农摩崖石刻六字真言（四）

磨房沟摩崖石刻

石刻位于德钦县佛山乡鲁瓦村委会梅里石村民小组北面河沟。河沟为东西走向，西高东低，地势陡峭，河水源自西边的梅里雪山，经此流入澜沧江。卡瓦格博外转道经此。摩崖石刻分布在河沟南面崖壁上。根据经文内容和风化程度以及其他迹象推测，此处藏文摩崖石刻最初形成时间约为元代。随着转经路线的确定和延续，石刻随之堆积，形成今天如此大规模的藏文石刻群。直到今天，还有石刻艺人不断在崖壁上刻绘。

磨房沟摩崖石刻（一）

磨房沟摩崖石刻（二）

磨房沟摩崖石刻（三）

丹达河摩崖石刻

石刻位于德钦县羊拉乡，在海拔2536米的丹达河桥东岸一堵约1000平方米的崖壁上，密密麻麻刻满了藏文经咒，除了六字真言外，还有大量的其他咒语

丹达河口摩崖石刻全貌

丹达河摩崖石刻六字真言（一）

丹达河摩崖石刻六字真言（二）

丹达河摩崖石刻六字真言（三）

丹达河摩崖石刻局部

达摩祖师洞石刻

达摩祖师洞石刻位于维西县塔城乡其宗村东面约6公里的高山上。达摩祖师洞及其周围有众多的历史文化遗迹和宗教圣迹，保存完好。在众多遗物和遗迹中，数量最多、文化内涵最丰富、价值最高的是石刻。这些石刻可以分为摩崖石刻和嘛呢石刻两类。

达摩祖师洞小转经道内所有裸露的岩石上都刻满了藏文经文，中转经道和大转经道旁以及达摩山脚的春独坝和茶马古道旁的岩石上也刻有大量藏经文。

达摩祖师洞经谷里有108座嘛呢石堆，另有上百座嘛呢石刻散堆在祖师洞道路口、寺院旁或镶嵌在佛殿墙壁上。这批石刻主要由文字石刻和造像石刻两种：文字石刻有藏文、梵文和汉文三种，内容主要是经文咒语，数量最多的是《大般若经》《金刚经》和六字真言，还有部分记事和村规民约等内容的藏文石刻；造像石刻内容主要是佛、菩萨、护法神、山神、高僧大德、灵兽珍禽及一些符号。

石刻的雕刻手法丰富多彩，有线刻、减地阳刻、浅浮雕、高浮雕、雕刻施彩等，或纯以白描或多种刻法并用。虽出自民间，可石刻风格多样、造型丰富、构图考究、技法娴熟，刀法精练，精美绝伦。

达摩祖师洞记事石刻

达摩祖师洞嘛呢石刻三狮图（一）

达摩祖师洞嘛呢石刻三狮图（二）

达摩祖师洞嘛呢石刻六字真言

香格里拉仙人洞摩崖石刻

在香格里拉大峡谷前往稻城亚丁的河谷两岸峭壁上有香格里拉最大的喀斯特溶洞——赤土仙人洞。洞口石壁上天生一个脚印，五指俱全，被视为世间少有的奇特景象。

仙人洞摩崖石刻六字真言

仙人洞吉努谷摩崖石刻十一面观音像

仙人洞吉努谷摩崖石刻摩尼宝、六字真言

香格里拉市康斯摩崖石刻

康斯摩崖石刻全景

康斯摩崖石刻酥油灯

康斯摩崖石刻局部

香格里拉市侧庸摩崖石刻

侧庸摩崖石刻局部（一）

侧庸摩崖石刻局部（二）

德钦县嘛呢石刻

德钦县嘛呢石刻（一）

德钦县嘛呢石刻（二）

德钦县嘛呢石刻（三）

德钦县嘛呢石刻（四）

德钦县嘛呢石刻（五）

德钦县阿东嘛呢石刻

德钦县久农嘛呢石刻

德钦县羊拉嘛呢石刻

维西县嘛呢石刻

维西县塔城关嘛呢石刻佛祖像

维西县其宗嘛呢石刻四壁观音

维西县塔城关嘛呢石刻

维西县巴迪嘛呢石刻四臂观音像

维西县巴迪嘛呢石刻夏琼像

香格里拉市嘛呢石刻

香格里拉市嘛呢石刻（一）

香格里拉市嘛呢石刻（二）

香格里拉市嘛呢石刻（三）

香格里拉市嘛呢石刻（四）

香格里拉市嘛呢石刻（五）

香格里拉市嘛呢石刻（六）

香格里拉市嘛呢石刻（七）

香格里拉市嘛呢石刻（八）

香格里拉市嘛呢石刻（九）

香格里拉市嘛呢石刻（十）

后记

我们长期从事云南少数民族古籍的抢救保护、翻译整理和出版规划工作，对云南少数民族古籍的分布、储量和传承现状有一个基本的了解，发现各民族都拥有或历史上曾经拥有过一些载体独特、形式各异的非纸质典籍，全面抢救保护、搜集整理这些分布零散、濒临消失且长期不被关注的少数民族非纸质典籍是一项具有重要意义的文化工程。

2015 年初，我们便逐步对各民族的非纸质典籍开展专题调查，不断征集线索、采集古籍图片，随着资料的不断累积，便萌生了将非纸质典籍专题影印出版的想法。这个想法得到云南人民出版社的大力支持，经申报入选“国家民文出版项目库”，并获民族文字出版专项资金的经费支持，为编纂出版本书创造了有利的条件。2017 年，本书主创团队参与云南大学周琼教授主持的国家社会科学基金重大项目“中国西南少数民族灾害文化数据库建设”，进一步推动了本项目的执行。

抢救保护承载着丰富民族文化内涵的云南少数民族非纸质典籍，具有重要的意义，也是一个充满挑战和未知的尝试。全面搜集云南各少数民族的非纸质典籍是一项耗时费钱费力的工作，这些典籍东一本西一样地散布在全省各地，从线索征集到一一获得授权采集图片确实经历了各种波折。

有的图片在采集过程中受自然条件的限制，采集难度较大。特别是金石铭刻类的图片，有的稍模糊，或缺乏全景图，甚是遗憾。图片如愿采集回来了，要将这些琳琅满目的典籍进行鉴别、释读、分类更是一项艰巨的任务，没有统一的划分标准可以参照、没有现成的经验可资借鉴，我们唯有摸着石头过河。进入统稿、编排环节，我们既要考虑覆盖云南各世居少数民族，又要考虑丛书的体量、编排等，取舍两难，着实让人困扰。最后，我们唯有以抢救保护、搜集整理少数民族古籍资料为出发点，以云南少数民族非纸质典籍的文化价值作为评判标准，以期为社会科学研究、文化产业发展等提供可资借鉴的材料。就收录范围，我们采用广义的民族古籍概念，适当突破民族古籍学学科的界定和范围，各民族的金石铭刻、骨刻、丝帛素书、竹木简牍等都是我们收录的对象，而结绳记事、刻木记事、树叶信等族属不明、内涵不清、争议较大的暂不作收录。所收录典籍的时间下线统一为1949年以前。就典籍的考释和图解，目前学界对各民族古籍的搜集整理、研究程度参差不齐，对古籍的翻译整理和释读等亦有巨大差距。如对纳西族非纸质典籍的收集、研究起步较早，我们基本可以释读典籍的名称和内容。但彝、壮、藏、傣等民族的非纸质典籍研究尚处于起步阶段，释读、命名尚有难度，如壮族的骨刻书，我们知道是用于历算的，但具体的内涵、使用方法尚未形成统一定论，我们实不敢妄解。所以部分非纸质典籍的文字说明略显简单粗陋。

本项目得到了云南人民出版社的大力支持和配合，特别是金学丽编审在项目策划、调研、稿件甄选、编辑等方面倾注了很多的心血，为项目的顺利开展做出了巨大的努力。吴贵飙馆长、普学旺译审、谢沫华研究馆员、起国庆研究馆员在项目申报、执行等方面给予了切实可行的指导意见和帮助。

本书资料的收集，得到丽江市东巴文化研究院、丽江市博物院、丽江玉龙纳西族自治县图书馆、迪庆藏族自治州藏学研究院、文山壮族苗族自治州民族宗教事务局等基层民族古籍工作部门的全力支持和配合，得到李德静、牛增裕、木琛、李瑞山、王珺、王明富、和树军、旦正太、唐新强、和丽宝、赵庆莲、陆保成、依旺的等专家的鼎力相助，谨致谢意。

为较好地呈现这套丛书，我们多方求证、全面搜集典籍、认真编排，确实做了很多切实的努力。但鉴于本书的执行、撰稿人员以青年学者居多，书稿难免有考虑不周和不当之处，敬请读者批评指正！

本书编委会

2018年12月

Postscript

We have been engaging in the rescue, protection, translation, sorting and publication planning of ancient books and records of ethnic minorities in Yunnan for a long time, and have a basic understanding on the distribution, reserves and inheritance status of ancient books and records of ethnic minorities in Yunnan. We find that all the ethnic minorities have or once had some non-paper ancient books and records with unique carriers and various forms in history. It is a cultural project of great significance to comprehensively rescue, protect, collect and sort out these scattered non-paper ancient books and records of ethnic minorities that are on the verge of disappearance and have not been drawing attention to for a long time.

We began to conduct special investigations on non-paper ancient books and records of various ethnic minorities, and are constantly collecting clues and pictures of ancient books and records since the beginning of 2015. With the continuous accumulation of data, we came up with the idea of photocopying and publishing special subjects of non-paper ancient books and records. This idea was vigorously supported by Yunnan People's Publishing House, and it was selected into the "national project library for publication of ethnic books and records" through application. Besides, it was also supported by the special fund for the publication of the ethnic books and records, and has created favorable conditions for compilation and publication of this book. In 2017, the creative team of this project participated in "the Establishment of the Database for Disaster Culture in the Ethnic Minorities in Southeast China" (Approval Number of the Project: 17ZDA158) which is the major project of the national social science foundation, and vigorously promoted the implementation of this series of books.

It is of great significance to rescue and protect the non-paper ancient books and records of ethnic minorities in Yunnan, which carries over rich ethnic cultural connotations, and is also an attempt full of challenges and mysteries. It is a time-consuming, costly and arduous task to collect all the non-paper ancient books and records of ethnic minorities in Yunnan. These ancient books and records are widely scattered all over the province. Relevant working personnel have experienced various twists and turns from collecting the clues to obtaining the authorization to collect pictures one by one. Restricted by the natural conditions, some pictures are difficult to take. In particular, the inscription pictures are slightly blurred or lack of panoramic images. What a pity! At last, the pictures were collected as expected. It is an arduous task to identify, interpret and classify these dazzling records. There is no unified classification standard to refer to and no ready-made experience to base on. We have to grope our way. In terms of compilation and arrangement, not only should we consider the coverage of ethnic minorities living in Yunnan, but also we should take the volume and arrangement of the series of books into account. It is really confusing to make choices. Finally, we can only take the rescue, protection, collection and sorting-out of the ancient books and records of ethnic minorities as the starting point, and the cultural value of non-paper ancient books and records of ethnic minorities in Yunnan as the evaluation standard, so as to provide reference materials for social science research and cultural industry development. In terms of the scope of inclusions, we adopt the broad concept of ethnic ancient books and records and appropriately break through the definition and scope of ethnic ancient books and records. Inscriptions, bone carvings, silk books and bamboo and wooden engravings of various ethnic minorities are all included in our collection scope, while the records of rope knotting, wood carving and leaf letters are not included for the time being due to their unclear and controversial connotations. The lower limit of time of the ancient books and records collected is uniformly fixed as prior to 1949. In terms of the interpretations and illustrations of ancient books and records, collection, collation and research on ancient books and records of various ethnic minorities are at different levels, and there is a huge gap in the translation, collation and interpretation of ancient books and records. For instance, due to early start of the collection and research on the Naxi non-paper ancient books and records, we can basically read names and contents of the ancient books and records. However, the research on non-paper ancient books and records of the Yi, Zhuang, Tibetan, Dai and other ethnic minorities is still in the initial stage, and it is difficult to read and name them. For example, we know that the bone carvings of the Zhuang Ethnic Minority are used for calendar calculation, but no unified conclusion has been reached on their specific connotation and method of use. We don’t dare to make improper interpretations. Therefore, some of the explanatory notes on the non-paper ancient books are slightly simple and not so detailed.

This project has received vigorous support and cooperation from Yunnan People's Publishing House. In particular, Senior Editor Jin Xueli has spared no efforts in project planning, research, manuscript selections and editing, and made a great contribution to the smooth development of the project. Director Wu Guibiao, senior translator Pu Xuewang, Research librarian Xie Mohua and Qi Guoqing have provided practical guidance and help in the project application, implementation and other aspects.

Data collections for this book has been completely supported and cooperated by the Research Institute of Dongba Culture of Lijiang, the Library of Yulong Naxi Autonomous County of Lijiang, the Research Institute of Tibetan Studies in Diqing Prefecture, the Affairs Bureau of Ethnic and Religious Affairs of Zhuang-Miao Autonomous Prefecture of Wenshan and other grass-roots departments of ethnic ancient books and records. We would like to express our gratitude to Li Dejing, Niu Zengyu, Mu Chen, Li Ruishan, Wang Jun, Wang Mingfu, He Shujun, Dan Zhengtai, Tang Xinqiang, He Libao, Zhao Qinglian, Lu Baocheng, Yi Wangdi and other experts.

We have made lots of practical efforts in seeking confirmations from various sources, comprehensively collecting ancient books and records and making arrangements carefully, so as to better present this series of books. However, since the book is mainly collected and compiled by young scholars, it is hard to avoid making incomprehensive and improper considerations. We are looking forward to your criticism and corrections!

Editorial Board of the Book

December, 2018